England has always been regarded as the birthplace of trade unionism yet the oldest existing trade union document is the 1788 minutes book of the Belfast Cabinetmakers' Club. The records of the Irish Parliament show that there were 'combinations' of workmen in early eighteenth century Dublin — a law to ban them was passed in 1729.

Severe laws, the pillory and the birch failed to suppress the rising tide of Irish trade unionism. It survived and its emergence is interwoven with the political history of the country. Daniel O'Connell in his day was an enemy. So was Parnell: 'What is trade unionism but the landlordism of labor? I would not tolerate, if I were at the head of government, such bodies as trade unions.' Michael Davitt, on the other hand, promoted them. At the beginning of this century Jim Larkin became a world symbol of Labour leadership. The Irish Citizen Army formed by James Connolly and members of the ITGWU joined the Republican Army in the rising in 1916. In 1918 the Irish Trades Union Congress organised a general strike against conscription. In Northern Ireland, a few of the more dedicated trade unionists have, for generations, fought an almost hopeless battle against the corrupting influence of the Unionist Party and the Orange Order.

The Irish were also prominent activists in the trade union movement abroad. In England Fergus O'Connor led the Chartists. John Doherty from Donegal was a pioneer union leader in Manchester. Robert Smillie of Belfast became leader of the Scottish coalminers, while the Fenian Frank Roney was for years a union organiser in California.

'Fascinating in its insights into Irish history'
— *The Irish News.*

Cover: Jim Larkin in Dublin, 1923

D1258675

ANDREW BOYD

The Rise of the Irish Trade Unions

ANVIL BOOKS

First published by Anvil Books in 1972
Reprinted 1976
This edition 1985

British Library Cataloguing in Publication Data

Boyd, Andrew, *1921*–
    The rise of the Irish trade unions.—[2nd ed.]
    1. Trade-unions—Ireland—History
    I. Title
    331.88′09415   HD6670.3
    ISBN   0-900068-21-3

Printed in Ireland by Mount Salus Press

CONTENTS

PREFACE TO THE SECOND EDITION

THE Rise of the Irish Trade Unions has been a popular book since it was first published in 1972. It has provided the reading public, those trade union members who are interested in the origins and traditions of their movement, and students of social history in many colleges and universities with an account of the Irish trade unions' long struggle for their political and industrial rights.

The Rise of the Irish Trade Unions also came as a surprise to many of these people who, bedazzled by the spectacular though brief career of Jim Larkin in the early years of this century, imagined that the Irish trade union movement began with the formation of the Irish Transport and General Workers' Union in 1909. But, as this book shows, the history of trade unions in Ireland goes back two hundred years before Larkin. The early struggles of the Irish trade unions against employers and parliament in the eighteenth century were every bit as exciting as Larkin's Belfast carters' strike in 1907, or his prolonged contest with the Dublin employer, William Martin Murphy, in 1913.

The Irish Parliament was legislating against the trade unions when Jonathan Swift was writing *Gulliver's Travels* and when Grattan's Parliament was demanding legislative independence. There were trade unions during the time of the United Irishmen. Forty years later trade unions were to be denounced and repudiated by Daniel O'Connell. The Irish trade unions emerged in the mid-nineteenth century to play their part in what were called the New Model Unions. In 1918 the Irish Trades Union Congress organised a general strike against conscription in Ireland. Altogether it is an extraordinary record of organisation and agitation.

During all these years many notable Irishmen, having gained experience of union organisation in their own country, were to emigrate, and pioneer trade union movements in Britain, in the United States of America, in Australia, and in the other English-speaking countries then in the British Empire. Among these pioneers were men like John Doherty from Buncrana in County Donegal, Robert Smillie of Belfast, Willam Allen from Carrickfergus, and Frank Roney who, as a young member of the Fenian Brotherhood, was compelled to emigrate to the USA and forbidden ever to return to Ireland.

When *The Rise of the Irish Trade Unions* first appeared I was reminded by Mrs Marie Johnston of Dublin of the part played by her husband, Thomas Johnston, in the Irish Labour Party and in the Irish Trades Union Congress during the early years of this century. Before the First World War, Tom and Marie Johnston lived for nearly twenty years in Belfast. They, along with D. R. Campbell, president of the Belfast Trades Union Council, toured the North of England on behalf of the ITGWU in 1913, and were able to persuade British trade unions and co-operative societies to send shiploads of food and clothing to the Dublin trade unionists "locked-out" by William Martin Murphy. Tom Johnston was General Secretary of the Irish TUC during the anti-conscription strike. He was the leader of the first group of Labour TDs in Dail Eireann.

Johnston was from England originally, but he understood the economic and political problems of Ireland better than most other Englishmen. Somewhat in the traditions of James Connolly, he could foresee the role of the trade unions and the Labour Party in helping to create a new Ireland in which there would be less poverty, less unemployment and less social distress, and from which fewer Irish people of the younger generations would want to emigrate.

It is possible that all this — and maybe much more — would have been achieved if Ireland had not been partitioned in 1920. This history of Ireland since then, and particularly the history of the trade unions and Labour parties, seems to vindicate James Connolly's prediction that partition would "set back the wheels of progress" and disrupt the oncoming unity of Irish Labour.

The twelve years, 1972–1984, have been years of stress and of challenge to the Irish trade unions, especially in the North of Ireland. Unemployment has risen so relentlessly throughout the whole country that by December 1984 there were 344,846 people altogether out of work.

Furthermore, inflation has placed all trade unions in difficult and defensive positions, so that all their energies are today concentrated on maintaining the living standards of their members against continually rising prices and the constant erosion of the real value of wages.

In addition to this, new laws have been passed in the United Kingdom (including Northern Ireland) restricting the rights won by the trade unions in generations of struggle and agitation.

Finally, fifteen years of communal turmoil and violence in Northern Ireland has been a terrible experience for most trade unionists who live there. Prominent union members like Senator Paddy Wilson of Belfast and Pat Campbell of Banbridge have been butchered by Loyalist murderers. Catholic workmen, most of them trade union members, have been forced to leave their employment in the Belfast shipyards and in other places where the Loyalists can exert force. Trade unions themselves are not warlike or militaristic organisations. So militarily they are no match for terrorist movements. The fact, moreover, that such movements draw most of their recruits from the working class ghettoes is an indication of how politically weak the trade unions in Northern Ireland have become. This weakness was nowhere more clearly revealed than at the time of the general strike called by the Ulster Workers' Council in 1974.

These, and other matters, are considered in more detail in the additional chapter which has been written for this edition.

And so, I present this second edition of *The Rise of the Irish Trade Unions*, confident that it will be as successful as the first edition and that it will continue to inform the younger generations in Ireland of the part played by the trade unions in the social and political history of their country.

Andrew Boyd   *Belfast, Spring 1985*

INTRODUCTION

FEW books have been written about the history of the trade unions in Ireland. Sidney and Beatrice Webb, who wrote the history of trade unionism in Britain, refer only briefly to the Irish unions. They describe them as "having emerged from handicraftsmen's local clubs, some of which dated from the middle of the eighteenth century."

The Webbs had studied the evidence which leading Irish trade unionists, as well as policemen, magistrates and employers, gave to the parliamentary committees that investigated trade unionism in 1824 and again in 1838. They were convinced that "in the early years of the nineteenth century the Dublin trades were the best-organised in the Kingdom," but beyond that they did not search deeply into the history of the Irish trade unions.

In 1925 the American historian, J. Dunsmore Clarkson, published his *Labour and Nationalism in Ireland*. Though this book has not been widely read and there are few copies now available, it contains much material that is invaluable to the student of Irish Labour history. W. P. Ryan's book, *The Irish Labour Movement,* appeared in 1919 and was fairly well known to Irish trade unionists forty years ago.

There is also James Connolly's *Labour in Irish History*. This book is not, however, a history of Irish labour but a socialist's interpretation of the main events in Irish history and of the part played by the working people of town and countryside in the struggle for national independence.

In more recent years—that is, from about 1950—several well-known scholars have written on specific aspects and periods of Irish Labour history. D. W. Bleakley of Belfast was one of the first to undertake this work. His thesis, now in the library of the Queen's University, Belfast, traces the origins and growth of trade unionism in the North of Ireland, especially during the second half of the nineteenth century.

J. W. Boyle, who is now a professor of history at a Canadian university, has written upon the development of the Irish Labour movement between 1880 and 1906. Fergus D'Arcy of Dublin has studied the political activities of the Dublin trade unions between 1820 and 1850, while Rachel O'Higgins has dealt with the Irish Chartists, in Ireland and in England, during the 1830s and 1840s. And also on the political side John F. Harbinson has written the history of the Northern Ireland Labour Party and its relations with the trade unions between 1890 and 1949. A more recent work is *Daniel O'Connell and the Trade Unions*, by Patrick Holohan of Cork.

Among the other books on Irish Labour history are Desmond Greaves's *Life and Times of James Connolly; Fifty Years of Liberty Hall*, which is the history of the Irish Transport and General Workers' Union; Emmet Larkin's *James Larkin;* and a book entitled: 1913 *Jim Larkin and the Dublin Lock-out.* The late R. M. Fox, an English journalist who lived many years in Dublin, wrote several books on Irish Labour leaders. Among these are biographies of James Connolly, of Jim Larkin and of Louis Bennett, as well as a history of the Irish Citizen Army.

What has not before now been written is a short history of the Irish trade unions from their beginnings in the early eighteenth century to the present day. Such a history may, therefore, be of some interest to the average reader, to the active trade unionist and perhaps also to the younger students in the universities.

1

TRADE UNIONS IN
EIGHTEENTH CENTURY IRELAND

TRADE unions, or combinations of workmen as they were called in the early days, were unlawful under several acts of the Irish parliament. The earliest of these acts was passed in 1729, though Clarkson, in his book, refers to "combinations of workmen, artificers, and others" being illegal under Irish law, as under English law, since the sixteenth century.

Moreover, the term 'unlawful combination' did not apply only to organisations of workmen. When employers and workers combined for an unlawful purpose, as they did in the Irish coal-mining industry in the middle of the eighteenth century, their combination was outlawed and condemned by parliament.

An Irish act of 1756 was directed against mine-operators and workmen who conspired to defraud landowners of the royalties to which they were entitled from the mines. This act specified penalties for the punishment of people "who sent threatening letters, destroyed carriages, or maliciously set fire to outhouses, stacks of hay, corn, straw or turf, or to boats and ships."

The act of 1729 dealt with "unlawful combinations of workmen, artificers and labourers employed in the several trades of this Kingdom" but, as it originated in a complaint about the size of bricks, it also included a clause for the purpose of preventing "abuses in the making of bricks and to ascertain their dimensions."

Having settled the proper length and breadth for bricks and having decided that trade unions were unlawful, parliament proceeded to do something to protect wages. They stipulated that wages be paid in full and in ready cash.

This meant that employers were forbidden to deduct any money from a workman's wages to pay for beer, whiskey or other goods and provisions. They were also forbidden to pay any part of wages in goods or liquor or to withhold part of wages for any reason whatsoever. Any workman who did not receive his full wages in ready money had the right to appeal to the magistrates for redress.

The practice of not paying wages in full, or of paying in kind rather than in cash—'truck,' as it was called—was widespread among Irish employers. The Irish parliament was concerned about truck and as early as 1715 had passed a law to stop it.

But this law, like the one passed in 1729, was ineffective. The problem of truck was discussed again in 1745 when parliament fixed a fine of £10 as the penalty on those who refused to obey the law. Yet as late as 1838 a witness who appeared before a parliamentary committee that was then inquiring into the trade unions testified that when he was a joiner's apprentice in Dublin, in the early years of the century, he often saw such commodities as tea, whiskey, fine-toothed combs and soap being taken by workmen as part payment of their wages.

In 1831 the parliament of the United Kingdom, which then legislated for Britain and the whole of Ireland, passed the first effective law against the truck system. This law declared that "all contracts for hiring an artificer in which payment was to be made in any other way than in the current coin of the realm were illegal, null and void." It also stated that wages not fully paid in cash could be claimed anew and the employer compelled "to make a fresh payment in current coin."

The first of Ireland's anti-combination laws, the one passed by parliament in 1729, was largely ignored by the employers, and by the workmen as well. The employers persisted in paying wages in whatever way they liked; the workmen continued to form trade unions, to raise funds for the benefit of their unemployed comrades, and to impose restrictions on the admission of apprentices to the various trades.

These activities continued until, in 1743, parliament prohibited assemblies of "three or more persons for the purpose of making by-laws respecting journeymen, apprentices or servants." This prohibition was part of a law which also stated that the collecting of money for the support of unemployed journeymen or "on any other pretence" was unlawful. This law further stated that the owners of inns and taverns used for trade union meetings would be treated like "those who kept common bawdy houses" and fined £20 for each offence.

The act of 1743 was also ignored by the workers and so the campaign by parliament and by the employers against the trade unions continued. The employers resented and often vigorously resisted the unions' seemingly endless demands for more wages, shorter working hours, and strict limitations on the entry of apprentices into the trades.

Parliament, for its part, was jealous of voluntary organisations, such as the trade unions, which tried to improve the conditions of working people. Most of the Irish MPs were landlords or the lackeys of landlords. They took the view that the welfare of the nation was their sole responsibility. And this view persisted for a very long time. In 1891 Charles Stewart Parnell, leader of the Irish Parliamentary Party, a landlord and employer himself though an enemy of Irish landlordism, told Michael Davitt that if he were head of an Irish government he would not tolerate trade unions.

"Whatever has to be done for the protection of the working class," said Parnell, "should be the duty of the government."

In the eighteenth century upper-class and middle-class Irishmen looked on the trade unions with either contempt or suspicion. As the historian R. B. McDowell writes in *Irish Public Opinion* 1750–1800:

The average sensible man of the century approached social problems with two suppositions. The first was that the existing class division of society was the best possible mechanism for producing the maximum of comfort for the largest number; the second that one's place in the system was largely determined by moral qualities. So while he was ready to grant the poor were often miserable, he accepted economic non-equality as an axiomatic fact, and considered their misery to some extent as an outcome of the inadequate moral stamina which had lodged them in that stratum of society.

As a result of this outlook [Professor McDowell continues], one method for improving the circumstances of the poor was uniformly frowned upon. Eminent lawyers, members of parliament, radicals (including Lucas) and divines (Protestant and Catholic alike) denounced as leading to beggary and ruin combinations of workmen with the object of shortening hours or raising wages.

These political radicals, clergymen, MPs and eminent lawyers all believed that "increased wages resulted from the competition of capitalists seeking labour," and that consequently "a forced or unnatural increase tended directly to raise prices and so damaged the export trade." Furthermore, they would have argued, the disturbances caused by trade unions during strikes and demonstrations scared away manufacturers and businessmen.

One expression of this viewpoint was the sermon preached by Robert Law, Rector of St. Mary's Church in Dublin, in January 1780. Dr. Law, who wished that nothing would impede the freedom of trade which the Irish parliament had won from England, described the "combinations of journeymen and working mechanics" as "the greatest of all possible evils."

In his sermon, which later, at the request of his parishioners, he published in pamphlet form, he stated that the only purpose of the combinations was "to exact higher wages for labour—

iniquitous extortions" as soon as business anywhere showed signs of improvement. But the members of the combinations, according to Dr. Law, did not want the extra money merely to help their families or to buy the normal necessities of life.

It was certain, he said, that the wage increases would "be wasted in the most profligate idleness and drunkenness to the inevitable discredit and detriment of trade."

He also believed that as Ireland had freedom of trade there should be a free market in labour, with each workman having the right to sell his services at whatever wage satisfied him. And he trusted that parliament would "ever be averse to fixing a stated price on any man's labour, lest it should cramp the ingenuity or diligence of the deserving artisan."

Robert Law, however, was not entirely biased against the workmen. He denounced rack-renting landowners who, at every opportunity, "exacted unreasonable rents for land." He warned "masters and employers who justly exclaim against all combinations of journeymen" to be careful themselves not to enter into private arrangements "to defraud the labourer of his hire."

The average sensible man of the eighteenth century, like Dr. Law, was, therefore, convinced that trade union meetings, which were generally held in taverns and inns where 'ale and punch' flowed freely, were nothing but occasions of idleness and debauchery.

And from this the upper and middle classes concluded that the suppression of trade unionism was in the best interests of the working people. Nonetheless, the many attempts by parliament and by the employers to suppress the unions and to have them banned by law all failed. The trade union movement grew stronger.

In the eighteenth century, when the parliamentary franchise and membership of parliament were restricted to a small class of wealthy property-owners, aggrieved citizens had the right to present petitions to parliament. Combinations for the purpose of presenting petitions, even though they may have been combinations of workmen complaining about their wages and working conditions, were not regarded as unlawful.

For example, in 1749 several hundreds of journeymen broadweavers in Dublin complained, in a petition to the House of Commons, that "the want of settled prices for their labour was causing them great discouragement and distress." They also complained that their employers forced them to do servile work in addition to their normal work at the looms and that weavers who refused to work under these conditions were denied employment and "suffered to idle in a starving condition, or obliged to leave the Kingdom to seek work in foreign parts."

Upon receiving this petition the House of Commons resolved "to deter the said masters from imposing the said servile work upon the petitioners."

Knowing, however, that the labour laws already on the statute book were ineffective, parliament enacted no new measure to impose the terms of their resolution upon the weaving masters. But they did appoint a committee under the chairmanship of Sir Richard Cox "to inquire into the causes of the disputes and dissensions between the masters and journeymen of the several trades of this Kingdom, and to find the most proper and likely means to prevent them for the future."

Sir Richard Cox and his committee eventually reported that, so far as they could find out, the causes of the many disputes in industry were:

The heavy fines imposed by some employers on their journeymen,
Unreasonable deductions by masters for the use of tools,
The difficulty and neglect of executing the acts to prevent unlawful combinations of workmen.

And among the measures which the committee recommended were:

Magistrates should decide wage rates at the quarter sessions each year,
Protestant journeymen employed in any of the trades or manufacturers, who had served an apprenticeship of seven years, should be exempt from paying fines imposed by the corporations,
The existing laws against combinations of workmen should be amended and explained.

Parliament accepted Sir Richard Cox's report but did nothing more about it. No legislation followed.

Meanwhile, despite the hostility of the employers and the politicians, trade union activity was increasing, especially in the main towns like Dublin, Belfast and Cork.

Early in August 1752 the Dublin newspapers reported that, on the previous Sunday, three journeymen woolcombers had been brought before the magistrates for "riotously assembling with several others and unlawfully forcing away from their work such as would not come into their illegal combination."

It would seem, from these reports, that the woolcombers had been on strike and had set up pickets to prevent others from going to work in the strike-bound workshops.

The three journeymen were sent to Newgate prison and kept there for nearly twelve months. At the assizes the following July (1753) they were convicted for unlawful assembly and ordered by the court to be fined £5 and imprisoned for two months.

The convicted men appealed to the City Assembly, saying that they were starving in jail, and begged that the fines be remitted. The Assembly upheld their appeal and released them after they had promised to be of good behaviour for the next three years.

It is recorded in the minutes of the City Assembly that, a few days after the journeymen woolcombers had been released, James Lacey, a master hosier, claimed that he had been "put to great expense in prosecuting and convicting several journeymen hosiers for entering into an unlawful combination to raise their wages and lessen their hours of work." Lacey claimed reimbursement of this expenditure and was given £20 by the City Treasurer. The money was raised from fines imposed upon the men whom Lacey had prosecuted.

In 1757 parliament, pestered no doubt by seemingly endless complaints and petitions from employers, imposed further penalties on workmen who formed trade unions. Acts which were passed during that year laid down terms of imprisonment varying from three to six months on anyone convicted of "swearing or being sworn into a combination to raise the prices usually paid for weaving." These acts referred mainly to the hemp and linen trades but they were so worded that they could have been invoked against trade unions in any industry.

Another law, passed in 1763, provided that anyone "attempting to fix the price of labour, either by calling a meeting, making rules, or preventing others from working, should, on conviction, be sent to prison for six months and thrice whipped." This act contained ninety-seven clauses but nowhere, except in a section which restricted the employment of apprentices, did it offer any protection to workmen.

The pillory and the birch were common forms of punishment for active trade unionists in the eighteenth century. In his *History of the Dublin Bakers and Others* John Swift writes that "around 1770 there was much activity on the part of the authorities against combining workmen."

On 3 January 1770 two weavers were found guilty of forming a trade union and were whipped through the streets from Newgate prison to College Green. The whipping was done by the public hangman while the High Sheriff of Dublin walked alongside to see that the punishment was fully carried out.

A month later the newspapers reported that the High Sheriff, accompanied by several master tailors, raided a number of houses where journeymen tailors were supposed to have been holding union meetings. The sheriff and his posse took away "books, boxes and money" and arrested a number of the tailors, three of whom were accused of being union leaders and were promptly thrown into Newgate prison.

A few weeks later, in March, Thomas Tennent, who kept a public house in Winetavern Street, was sentenced to be pilloried at the City Hall for allowing his premises to be used as a meeting place by the journeymen tailors.

A few years before this incident, in the early 1760s, the first Irish trade union to be identified by name appears in the records. This union was the Regular Carpenters of Dublin which, according to evidence which was given to a parliamentary committee in 1824, was founded in 1764. The Regular Carpenters were bound by twenty-three rules. These rules showed that the main purposes of the society were to support its sick members when they lost work through illness, to bury the dead, provide for the widows of deceased members, to raise money to finance litigation between journeymen carpenters and their employers, and to regulate the wages which the journeymen were entitled to be paid. Another rule required the union to provide apprenticeships for four pauper boys each year.

Patrick Farrell, a union leader who gave evidence to the 1824 committee on behalf of the Regular Carpenters, said that the union held its meetings quarterly—on Easter Monday, Whit Monday, First Monday in August and on St. Stephen's Day. These meetings were known as 'fields' because they were held in what were regarded as safe places outside the city, well beyond the boundaries in which the magistrates and high sheriffs operated. The business on the agenda was usually the state of the trade, wages and working conditions and the general grievances of members.

In 1891 the Regular Carpenters of Dublin merged with the carpenters' union in Britain and is now a section of the large union known throughout Great Britain and Ireland as the Amalgamated Society of Woodworkers.

In its earliest days the Dublin carpenters' union was also called the United Brothers of St. Joseph and, according to the history of the Amalgamated Society of Woodworkers, claimed to have been connected with the mediaeval Dublin Company of Carpenters, Millers, Masons and Tylers. There is, however, no evidence to support this claim. It seems to be based on fantasy rather than on historical fact. The Dublin Company of Carpenters was a guild of employers and continued as such until 1840, by which time, if Patrick Farrell's evidence can be relied upon, the Regular Carpenters of Dublin had been nearly eighty years in existence as a trade union of working journeymen.

At first, parliament was concerned mainly about the activities of trade unionists in Dublin which was the capital city and the main centre for trade, but soon after the report of Sir Richard Cox's committee, in 1749, the attention of the House of Commons was drawn to the existence of combinations in Cork.

From the little evidence available it seems that there were several unions active in Cork in the middle of the eighteenth century. They were accused, from time to time, of organising strikes, picketing, destroying tools, materials and machinery, and of ostracising employers who would not give in to their demands, as well as workmen who worked for less than the union rates of pay.

After considering a petition from the employers of Cork, parliament declared that anyone in the city of Cork who was found guilty of being a member of an unlawful trade union should "be imprisoned not above six months, whipped in public, and released only on giving recognisance of good behaviour for seven years."

Parliament then proceeded to impose a strict wages policy on Cork, on the assumption that such a policy would stop the spread of trade unionism. The application of this wages policy was left to the magistrates who, at the Easter sessions each year and in the presence of the City Recorder or his deputy, would decide "what wages or sum of money every mason, carpenter, slater, cooper or other artificer shall take and be paid by the day or by the certain denomination, piece or parcel of work or job, either with or without meat and drink during the year following."

The law further stated that if any workman forced his employer to pay wages higher than the rates decreed by the magistrates the money would be forfeited. One half of it would be paid to the local workhouse and the other half to the person who brought the prosecution.

Parliament realised, however, that it would be very difficult to detect and convict those who formed themselves into trade unions. "Unlawful assemblies are usually held secretly and in private places," said the House of Commons. And so they took special measures to encourage informers and to protect the informers when they gave evidence under oath against the unions.

2

CLASS WAR AND DEMONSTRATIONS

IN the eighteenth century the trades of Dublin were still regulated by guilds that had been set up in the Middle Ages; but whereas the mediaeval guilds had been fraternities of masters, journeymen and apprentices, the guilds of the eighteenth century were controlled entirely by the masters, who alone claimed the right to be called guildsmen.

The journeymen were excluded from membership of the guilds and forced often to work under conditions that would today be considered equal to slavery or serfdom. And when they formed trade unions for the purpose of improving their wages and conditions of employment they met with the most determined opposition of the guildsmen. Parliament passed laws against the unions; the masters of the guilds supported and supplemented these laws with their own rules and resolutions.

John J. Webb, in his book, *The Guilds of Dublin*, records the decision of the Masters, Warden and Brethren of the Corporation of Barbers, known also as the Guild of St. Mary Magdalen, to suppress a union that had been formed by the journeymen barbers and wigmakers for the purpose of "lessening their usual hours of work."

Thomas Wood, master of this guild, called a meeting on 10 October 1757 and placed several propositions or motions before his members. The guild then resolved, "having taken into consideration the evil tendency and iniquity of all unlawful combinations and in order to put an immediate stop thereto," that:

Any master barber or perukemaker that shall employ any journeyman who, between the 29 September and the 25 March each year, shall refuse to work at the trade from the hour of seven in the morning until nine at night, and who, from the 25 March to the 29 September each year, shall refuse to work at the trade from six o'clock in the morning until sunset, shall for every offence, forfeit and pay the sum of £1.19.11.

Any master who shall employ any journeyman who has been discharged for refusing to work the hours above-mentioned shall, for every offence, forfeit and pay the like sum of £1.19.11.

Any master who shall employ any journeyman without first inquiring from the master with whom such journeyman last wrought the reasons for his parting with such journeyman and whether such journeyman has given a week's notice to his former master shall be fined the sum of £1.19.11.

A fine was also to be imposed on any guildsmen who offered higher wages to journeymen already employed by other masters or who negotiated with his own journeymen about higher wages.

By these resolutions the guild was obviously encouraging employers to keep a black-list of active trade unionists and to see that these men were not given jobs. It was also restricting the right of journeymen to move to better-paid positions within the trade and at the same time preventing free negotiations between workmen and employers about wages and working conditions.

The guild's next resolution was against enhanced hourly payments for overtime. It stated that "all journeymen that are longer employed than the usual time shall be paid for such extraordinary hours the same, in proportion, as for the day."

Finally, the guild resolved to "prosecute to the utmost rigour of the law all journeymen of the trade who shall enter into unlawful assemblies or combinations" as well as the owners of houses wherein these combinations held their meetings.

They also agreed to "give all due consideration to such persons" as would give them information.

These resolutions were not idle threats because a year later, in 1758, the guild assisted James Gaynor, who is described in the records as 'a mere quarter-brother or junior guildsman,' when he prosecuted his journeymen for forming an unlawful combination.

Some years later, in 1769, the Lord Mayor of Dublin received what he considered an alarming memorandum from certain members of the City's Common Council. The memorandum stated that:

. . . an outrageous mob have of late entered into unlawful combinations, particularly the weavers, bakers, and coopers of this city; they have quit the work of their respective employers for the purpose of advancing their wages, and have committed many acts of violence. . . .

J. J. Webb has explained that "the Common Council were sternly opposed to combinations of journeymen formed for the purpose of improving their conditions of employment," and that the guilds had "a preponderating influence on the Common Council."

The memorandum from the Council to the Lord Mayor in 1769 was, therefore, really a complaint of the combined Dublin employers against the trade unions. Upon receiving the memorandum the Lord Mayor decided to offer a reward for information that would lead "to the conviction of the persons concerned in the said unlawful combinations."

The following year, 1770, the master tailors prosecuted their journeymen for forming a union, and afterwards complained to the Common Council that the case had cost them twenty guineas in legal fees. The tailors asked the council for financial help; otherwise, they said, they could not continue with the good work of suppressing trade unions.

The council members had no objection whatever to giving money for this purpose. In fact they agreed that the master tailors be given a hundred guineas to help them promote a bill in parliament "for preventing irregular risings among journeymen tailors and for regulating the hours of their work and their wages."

The council was also concerned about the spread of trade unionism among the journeymen coopers who, like everybody else, had been asking for higher wages and shorter hours of work.

The master coopers, not wishing to yield to these demands, were, as they told the council, "obliged to invite workmen from other parts of the Kingdom."

These imported workmen—'colts' as they were called by Dublin's trade unionists—came under attack from the men whom they displaced. One of them, an Englishman by the name of John Dinan, was so badly injured that "many pieces were taken out of his skull." He got ten guineas by way of compensation from the council. The council also offered a reward of twenty guineas for information that would lead to the prosecution and conviction of those who attacked Dinan.

Meanwhile the master tailors, whose guild was known as the Master Taylors and Staymakers of the City of Dublin, used the money they had been given by the council to prepare a case against the union. On 18 February 1772 they presented a petition to parliament, their main complaint being that many of their journeymen had gone on strike. As the petition put it:

. . . the journeymen had departed from the service of their masters without just cause, and had entered into combinations to advance their wages to unreasonable prices and to lessen their hours of work.

The master tailors also asserted that the demands of the journeymen "were greatly to the prejudice of the tailoring and staymaking trades." They believed that these demands, if successful, would "encourage idleness and increase the number of poor in the city."

The masters also alleged that "the source of the disorders was clubs and societies formed and held in different parts of the city" and that within these clubs "associations were entered into, oaths administered, and other illegal acts committed."

One thing the master tailors resented was being forced, by the union, to pay a uniform rate of wages to all journeymen. They said that the union demanded "the same wages to the most skilful as to the most ignorant, without any regard being had to merit, ingenuity or industry."

Finally, they asked why the several acts of parliament had failed, until then, to prevent unlawful combinations of workmen.

This petition from the master tailors was passed to a special committee under the chairmanship of the Marquis of Kildare and, a week later, the marquis reported that "in the opinion of the committee the petitioners have fully proven the allegations of their petitions and deserve the aid of parliament."

Kildare's committee also considered a petition from the master shipwrights whose complaint was that the journeymen in the shipbuilding trade had formed a union. The committee decided that the master shipwrights also had cause for complaint.

Parliament then discussed these petitions along with the committee's reports and at the end of the debate decided there was need for a bill to regulate "the journeymen tailors and journeymen shipwrights of the City of Dublin and the Liberties thereof."

The act which parliament passed seemed merely to repeat and extend the penalties laid down in earlier laws. A fine of £20 or three months in jail was to be the punishment for any house-owner who allowed trade union meetings to be held on his premises. Workmen found guilty of taking part in union meetings were to be fined £10 or sent to jail for three months.

The act then fixed the hours of work in the tailoring and staymaking trades at twelve-and-a-half per day—from six o'clock in the morning until eight o'clock at night with one break of thirty minutes for breakfast and another break of one hour for dinner.

It also fixed the wages of journeymen tailors and staymakers at not less than one shilling and fourpence per day and not more than one shilling and eightpence. Workers who refused to work for these wages were to be fined £10 upon conviction. If they combined to force their employers to pay more than the rates laid down in the act, the fine was also £10 or three months in jail. Employers who offered wages higher than what parliament decreed broke the law and were liable to be fined £100.

And any agreement to pay wages above the legal rate was to be judged null and void.

The same act fixed the working day for shipwrights—from six o'clock in the morning until six o'clock in the evening, with the usual time off for meals. The shipwrights' wages were to be not less than two shillings a day and not more than two shillings and sixpence. And the same penalties, as in the case of the tailors and staymakers, were to be imposed on employers or workmen who broke the regulations.

Soon after the passing of this act a bill was brought in to prevent trade unionism in the building trades. The crafts listed for attention were the masons, bricklayers, slaters, stone-cutters, workers in stucco, plasterers, carpenters and painters. But the member of parliament who brought forward this bill died suddenly; parliament adjourned, and the bill was forgotten.

In February 1780 the House of Commons Grand Committee for Trade, under the chairmanship of Sir Lucius O'Brien, started on yet another inquiry into the trade unions. Two weeks earlier, on 22 January, one of the Dublin newspapers had reported that:

... as the most effective means to promote industry and extend the manufactures of this Kingdom, a bill is intended to be brought into parliament to regulate workmen ... and to prevent those destructive combinations that are the source of idleness, drunkenness and cruelty, and as the laws now in being have been found ineffectual such pains and penalties will be inserted in this bill as will give a new face to business.

By that time it was evident that employers and parliament, as the newspaper implied, had been quite unsuccessful in their many attempts to suppress the trade unions. Indeed as recently as 1776 a drive against the unions of tailors, cabinetmakers, brewers, tallow-chandlers, bakers, cotton-spinners, cutlers and carpenters in Dublin had failed.

At that time, however, the Patriot Party, led by Henry Grattan, was engaged in the campaign for free trade, i.e. for the removal of all the commercial restraints which the English parliament had imposed on Irish trade and industry. With the granting of free trade, in 1779, the Irish manufacturers renewed their demands for the suppression of the trade unions. They argued that Ireland's industries would enjoy the full advantages of free trade only if workmen were restrained in their demands for higher wages, compelled to accept new methods of production and persuaded to adopt more conciliatory attitudes towards their employers.

The manufacturers' case was that in the conditions of free trade the trade unions were obstacles to progress. They imposed unwarranted restrictions on the recruitment and training of labour, objected to improved methods of production and to labour-saving machines, and insisted on standard rates of pay.

But the working people had good reason for fearing the machines. There was widespread unemployment and poverty. In 1774, for example, about one-third of all the weavers in Ireland, apart from the people in other trades, were unemployed. Another 10,000 weavers had emigrated to America. Five years later, in February 1779, the Sheriffs of Dublin informed the Lord Lieutenant that there were 19,000 weavers in starvation in the city.

As the Industrial Revolution proceeded and machinery increasingly replaced skilled labour, handloom weavers and craftsmen in other trades were driven deeper into poverty.

In *The Irish Labour Movement* W. P. Ryan has described the plight of the weavers in Belfast as reported to the Select Committee on Hand Loom Weavers in 1835. John Boyd, who gave evidence to the committee, said that in Belfast and in the countryside nearby there were three classes of handloom weavers. The highest-paid and best-skilled could earn six shillings or six-and-sixpence a week for working between fourteen and eighteen hours each day. But only a small number earned these wages. The majority of the weavers got about five shillings or five-and-sixpence for the same hours. The worst off were the poorly-skilled. They worked only on the coarsest materials and could earn no more than three shillings or three-and-sixpence for a week's work.

James Hope, who had organised the Society of United Irishmen in the 1790s and who, with Henry Joy McCracken, had led the rebel army at the Battle of Antrim in '98, was one of the weavers who lived in Belfast in the mid-nineteenth century. He had survived the rebellion and had gone into hiding to escape arrest and punishment.

When Dr. R. R. Madden wrote the second series in *The Lives and Times of the United Irishmen* he described Hope as "a poor weaver, living in Belfast, not in absolute poverty but in very humble circumstances."

James Hope was probably not as poor as the weavers who earned six shillings a week and lived mainly on oatmeal porridge, boiled potatoes, a herring now and then, and a little bread, and whose main beverage was sour milk because they could afford to buy only half-an-ounce of tea and a half-pound of sugar each week.

The evidence given to the Select Committee on Hand Loom Weavers showed that the weekly household purchases for a weaver, his wife, and their two children were:

10 stone of coal at 1½d. per stone	1s.	3d.
¾ stone of oatmeal	1s.	3d.
2 pound of candles		9d.
3 stone of potatoes		7½d.
8 quarts of sour milk		4d.
8 herrings		4d.
½ ounce of tea and ½ pound of sugar		5½d.
bread		4d.
½ pound of soap		2½d.
	5s.	6½d.

The weaver had also to pay a shilling a week for the hire of the loom he worked, and a rent of maybe a shilling or one-and-sixpence for his house.

These poor people could exist only by sending their wives and children out to beg. A few had little patches of ground where they grew potatoes. And the poorest of them lived almost entirely on the potatoes they grew themselves, flavoured with a little salt.

Indeed many of them may have spent their lives weaving cloth in order to pay the rent of their potato patches. Thus they carried upon their backs two classes of exploiters: the weaving master who supplied them with yarn and took away the finished cloth, and the landowner whose piece of ground they rented.

The incomes of the handloom weavers were low because factory-weaving had overtaken their craft and because they were not organised in trade unions. This was borne out by a manu-facturer named Alexander Moncrieff who gave evidence to the committee. He said that in Belfast the sectarian differences between Catholics and Protestants had kept the handloom weavers from forming a union, though there had been a union of muslin-weavers in Belfast early in the nineteenth century.

In other trades, especially where many men worked together as in building or in workshops, craft unions resisted the bringing in of machines.

Typical, perhaps, of the trade unions' defensive attitude to machinery was the policy of the Ancient Corporation of Carpenters of the City of Cork. This old union merged into the Amalgamated Society of Carpenters and Joiners in 1892, but, for generations before that, it refused to allow its members to handle any materials prepared by machinery. The Ancient Corporation of Carpenters also defeated all efforts to introduce piecework into the trade, kept strict control of the number of apprentices and refused to work with non-union labour. It had the reputation of never having lost a trade dispute in its long history.

Employers from twenty different trades presented evidence to Sir Lucius O'Brien's committee and insisted that the trade unions be suppressed with the full vigour of the law.

Some of the employers described how the unions were organised, where they met, how the rules were made and contributions collected. Many of them alleged that workmen who refused to subscribe money to the unions were persecuted. They all denounced trade unionism as a form of tyranny, both on the employers and on the workmen.

The committee continued its investigations until the end of May. A few days later, at the beginning of June, O'Brien presented a bill for the suppression of all trade unions. The preamble to this bill described the unions as a public nuisance and declared that the magistrates and other law-enforcement officers should not hesitate to prosecute anyone suspected of union activities. The bill was duly passed by parliament, received the Royal assent, and became law in August of that same year.

Being directed against all trade unions, this Irish act of 1780 was far more far-reaching than any other labour law then on the statute book; it was twenty years ahead of Wilberforce's act which, in 1799, outlawed all the trade unions in Britain. It repeated many of the penalties laid down in earlier acts, removed all restrictions on the employment of apprentices, and declared that absence from work for any period longer than three days would be taken as evidence of trade union membership and punished accordingly.

The trade unions in Dublin had no intention, however, of allowing such a measure to pass through parliament unchallenged. In June they presented five different petitions against the bill to the House of Commons. They ran a press publicity campaign, paying for their own advertisements in the newspapers. They raised money and paid lawyers to plead their case before the House.

On 13 June, when the debate on the bill opened, 20,000 trade unionists, their families and their supporters assembled in

Phoenix Park and marched through the city to hand in their petitions at College Green. But apart from Hely Hutchinson, the member for Trinity College, the unions had no friends in parliament. The middle classes were hostile, the landlords antagonistic, and the newspapers printed long columns of anti-union comment.

The Irish Volunteers, from whom a more liberal attitude night have been expected, were also against the unions. Indeed during the year 1780 three corps of the Volunteers in Dublin passed resolutions which condemned the unions. On the day of the Phoenix Park demonstration the Dublin Corps turned out, at the request of the magistrates, to maintain law and order should rioting break out.

Sir Lucius O'Brien's act turned out to be just as ineffective as all the other statutes against the unions. Indeed within only a few months of its passing, the House of Commons had to consider the spread of trade unionism in the silk industry and in the provision trades. Again special laws were passed to regulate workmen in these trades.

During the summer of 1781 James Gandon, the English architect, started work on the construction of Dublin's Custom House, but he soon ran into trouble with the unions and was told by the local building craftsmen that only union labour could be employed on the contract. Gandon said that the workmen whom he had brought specially from England and from other parts of Ireland, outside Dublin, all had to join the unions. They each paid one guinea entrance fee and were told to work according to the unions' rules. There is no evidence, after that, to show that Gandon had any more serious labour trouble.

During the last twenty years of the eighteenth century the struggles between workers and employers, especially in Belfast and in Dublin, seem to have been very intense. And the unions, judging from the many denunciations to which they were subjected, were seldom the losers.

By the 1790s labour struggles had become so widespread that Judge William Downes, addressing the Dublin Grand Jury in 1795, denounced trade unionism in the following words:

... these combinations, notwithstanding the repeated efforts of parliament to suppress them, have increased in the most alarming manner and, at this moment, some important branches of industry are almost destroyed by them.

It was a common belief, held not only by Judge Downes but by many other people for a long time afterwards, that the trade unions were responsible for undermining and so destroying certain industries in Ireland. For example, the unions were accused of ruining the Dublin shipbuilding industry and the silk-weaving trade. This was stated by witnesses who gave evidence to the committee that inquired into trade unionism in 1824. But against this view Irish economic historians of the status of George O'Brien and E. J. Riordan have argued that the decline of many Irish industries was caused by the restrictions which Britain imposed after the Act of Union (1800). Thus the increasingly defensive activities of the Irish trade unions were most likely the result and not the cause of the decay of some Irish industries.

3

TRADE UNIONS IN THE REPUBLICAN NORTH

FROM the year 1788 comes the first evidence of trade union activity in Belfast. On 22 May that year a group of cabinet-makers started the Belfast Cabinetmakers' Club, the minutes-book of which is preserved at the headquarters of the Amalgamated Society of Woodworkers in London and is probably the oldest existing trade union document in the world. It is certainly, states the official history of the ASW, "the earliest authentic record of woodworkers' clubs."

Among the founders of the Belfast Cabinetmakers' Club, whose names are recorded in the minutes-book, was John Millar. He devoted many years of his life to trade unionism and, in 1810, his colleagues in the club acknowledged his services by voting him a 'free member' and settling on him a small pension, which they raised by a levy of twopence-halfpenny from each member every week.

The Belfast Cabinetmakers' Club drew up rules and by-laws and compiled lists of work-prices which the local employers were expected to observe. The club insisted, for example, that no employer should have more than two apprentices under training at any one time. Its members were told not to handle or finish chairs, bedposts or other items of furniture if imported, partly-built, from London.

Members of this union were involved in a dispute, in 1821, over non-unionism in one of the Belfast cabinetmaking firms. During this strike a non-union man called Wolfingden got a gunshot wound in the leg. He was not seriously injured but the shooting infuriated the local employers. Some 200 of them, mostly from outside the furniture trade, came together and offered a reward of £100 for information that would lead to the arrest and conviction of whoever shot Wolfingden.

During the 1790s Belfast went through a period when the trade unions were every bit as militant as they were in Dublin. On numerous occasions during that decade Belfast's carpenters, shoemakers, bricklayers, coopers, linen-weavers, cotton-weavers, as well as the workers in many other trades, issued demands for higher wages. And they were invariably ready to back these demands with strike action.

Strike threats and strike action seem to have been successful. For example, on 14 June 1792, the carpenters of Belfast announced in the columns of the *Northern Star,* a local republican newspaper, that they had managed to increase their wages to two shillings a day—twelve shillings a week.

But the *Northern Star,* despite its political radicalism and its association with the Society of United Irishmen, was anything but sympathetic to the unions. Indeed Samuel Neilson, proprietor and editor of the paper, repeatedly advised employers "not to yield to demands made in a tumultuous and illegal manner." On 9 June 1792 he published a letter which a number of local businessmen had sent to William Bristow, the Sovereign, or chief magistrate of Belfast. The letter asked Bristow to hold a meeting in the Town Hall so that the respectable people of Belfast "could take into consideration the present combinations that are forming among the different working tradesmen of this place."

In an editorial comment on this letter Neilson blamed the bricklayers, the carpenters, and especially the local cotton-weavers for organising and leading the trade unions. He again urged the employers to resist the unions' demands and called on Bristow to mobilise the local corps of Volunteers. "The Volunteers," he wrote, "have more than once obeyed the magistrates' call to enforce the law."

Neilson then reminded his readers that there were laws against trade unionism. He suggested that as working-class people were not in the habit of reading newspapers or consulting acts of parliament, a digest of these laws should be printed as a handbill and distributed throughout the town.

Perhaps even Neilson himself did not know how many labour laws there were because it would have taken more than one handbill to contain even a list of all the anti-combination laws then on the Irish statute book.

Meanwhile, Bristow, the Sovereign, arranged the meeting in the Town Hall, and, on Monday 11 June, a large number of employers, workmen and other citizens met to discuss the alleged menace of unlawful combinations.

Those who attended the meeting seemed mainly concerned with the demands of the muslin-weavers for more money. After a discussion that lasted most of the afternoon they decided to set up a committee of three employers, three weavers and three other citizens—an early joint industrial council, in fact—to study wages in the local cotton-weaving industry and suggest improvements.

This apparently satisfied the journeymen weavers—at least it satisfied those who were present at the meeting. But a few days later Bristow had to take Neilson's advice and call out the Volunteers. He was told that a large assembly of weavers had gathered in a field on the road to Lisburn and were threatening to wreck the houses of employers who refused to pay them more money.

Bristow rode out to where the weavers were assembled. He spoke to them and eventually convinced them that it would be wiser to go back home, forget all about violence and see what remedies the new committee would suggest. He feared, however, that there might be trouble and so he posted pickets of Volunteers in the streets of Belfast that evening and kept them on duty for several days.

One of the trade unions formed during the labour unrest of the 1790s was the Belfast Muslin Weavers' Society. This organisation was to be involved in a tragedy in 1817 when Gordon Maxwell, its president, was shot and mortally wounded. The attack took place on a Saturday evening when Maxwell was on his way from Belfast to Lisburn for a union meeting.

Maxwell lived for seven days after the attack and named John McCann, a local cotton employer, as the assailant. On this death-bed evidence McCann was brought to trial, but as his father and his brothers all swore he had not been anywhere near Lisburn on the night of the attack he was acquitted.

Members of the Belfast Muslin Weavers' Society may also have been implicated in the events which started at the house of Francis Johnston, an employer who lived at Peter's Hill, and which ended in the execution of two young men.

During the economic depression that followed the end of the wars with Napoleon—in 1815—Johnston tried to reduce the wages of his weavers. The weavers resisted. Some of them attacked Johnston's house and set it on fire.

Johnston retaliated by making more cuts and the workers again attacked his house. During this second attack someone threw a home-made bomb into Johnston's front parlour. No one was seriously injured but one of the attackers, probably the one who threw the bomb, had his thumb blown off. Next day the magistrates offered a reward of £200 for information that would lead to the arrest and conviction of the men responsible for the attack.

The year 1816 was a time of starvation, fever, and industrial distress in Belfast, and so the attack on Johnston's house was followed by rioting, looting and robbery throughout the town. The starving workers were driven to fury and violence by the knowledge that certain merchants in the town had hoarded vast quantities of food, in the hope that greater scarcity would raise prices. A group of the more humane citizens deplored this hoarding and called upon the magistrates to prosecute those who were guilty. The condition of the poor, these citizens pointed out, was really miserable, but this misery was made worse "by the avarice and extortions of huxters and forestallers" who, rather than sell their stocks at prevailing market prices, allowed them to rot in storehouses and cellars.

The first man arrested for the attack on Johnston's house was William Gray, the one who had had his thumb blown off. He turned informer and named five others—John Magill, John Doe, Joseph Madden, James Dickson and James Park—as his accomplices. These five men were brought to trial at Carrickfergus on 12 August 1816, with Gray as chief witness for the prosecution.

After a hearing that lasted all day, Park and Dickson were sentenced to eighteen months in jail and to be flogged in public. Magill, Doe and Madden were all sentenced to be hanged, but Madden, upon appeal to the Lord Lieutenant, had his sentence commuted to one of transportation for life. The death sentence on the other two stood, with execution fixed for Friday 6 September 1816. A reporter from the *Belfast News Letter* described how the sentences were carried out:

The convicts were taken from the jail at Carrickfergus about nine o'clock in the morning and put in a chaise. The attending clergymen were the Reverend Joseph Alexander, Reverend B. Mitchell, Reverend J. Stewart and Mr. Jonathan Blackwell. Behind the chaise followed two carts, one containing the apparatus for the gibbet and in it sat the executioner. The other cart was fitted up as a temporary scaffold and in it was another executioner brought from a distant county. He was disguised, having his head and face covered with black crepe. A strong military guard consisting of the Fifth Dragoons and several companies of the Royal Scots preceded and followed.

At noon this sombre procession reached Belfast where, at the upper end of High Street, a space had been cleared for the gibbet to be set up. And while a large crowd of spectators gathered, the two men, both still in their middle twenties, prayed with the clergy and received whatever last comfort they were offered. Then came the moment of execution.

John Doe was the first to be brought out. In his last words, read from the scaffold, he admitted that he had broken the law, but he claimed that he was not guilty of all the crimes with which he had been charged and for which he had been condemned to die. The last words of the other man, John Magill, were read to the crowd by the Reverend James Stewart.

Magill and Doe were hanged. After about thirty minutes, when the authorities were satisfied that they were dead, their bodies were taken down, put into two black coffins and carried across the Long Bridge into Ballymacarrett. They were buried next day, both in the one grave, in Knockbracken graveyard.

A week later Park and Dickson were brought to Belfast to be flogged in public. Park was first to be tied up. He received 314 lashes which, the local newspapers reported, the executioner inflicted with considerable effect. Dickson received 269 lashes. Both men were flogged unconscious, then dragged back to Carrickfergus jail to finish their terms of imprisonment.

During the last years of the eighteenth century the journeymen shoemakers of Belfast—and there were three hundred of them altogether—were very active trade unionists. They went on strike for higher wages in 1790, 1792, 1794 and 1799. Their employers, the master shoemakers, often advertised for workmen to take the places of those on the streets.

In the three years between 1799 and 1802 several journeymen, including two stonemasons, two coopers, six shoemakers and four carpenters, were sent to jail in Carrickfergus for forming trade unions in Belfast and demanding more money. In 1804 two bricklayers started a strike in Belfast and had to flee from the town to avoid arrest and imprisonment. Commenting on their flight the *Belfast News Letter* asked:

. . . what would become of the great works of elegance and utility, now being produced in our town, or contemplated, if such combinations were permitted?

Meanwhile, the Westminster House of Commons had passed a law, the Combination Act, which outlawed all trade unions. The author of this act was William Wilberforce, emancipator of the British Empire's black slaves and leader of a sect of Christian evangelists, known as the Clapham Set because Wilberforce lived at Clapham and held prayer meetings there. His attitude to the working people of England was, however, markedly different from his great concern for the chattel slaves. He deplored the tendency of workmen to form themselves into trade unions in order to improve their living standards. And he declared that unions were "a general disease in society" and should, therefore, be stamped out with such force that they would never rise again. During the twenty-five years when Wilberforce's act remained in force the magistrates, in all parts of Britain and Ireland, did their utmost, with fines and floggings and imprisonment, to wreck the unions.

Francis Place, known in history as 'the Radical Tailor of Charing Cross,' was one of the chief organisers of the campaign that eventually brought about the repeal of Wilberforce's law. Place believed that many magistrates far exceeded their powers when trade unionists appeared before them, and he wrote:

... could an accurate account be given of proceedings before magistrates, trials at sessions, and in the Court of King's Bench, the gross injustice, the foul invective and the terrible punishments inflicted would not, after a few years had passed, be credited on any but the best evidence.

In 1800 the Irish parliament, undermined by corruption, was abolished and Ireland came under the direct jurisdiction of Westminster. Presumably then Wilberforce's act should have applied in Ireland, but what actually happened was that, in 1803, Westminster passed an even more repressive law to deal with the Irish trade unions.

In Britain, for example, anyone convicted of being a member of a trade union was sent to prison for three months; in Ireland the sentence was six months. The penalty for collecting trade union contributions was £5 in Britain; in Ireland it was £10. The act covering Ireland also reimposed the numerous penalties contained in the acts passed by the Irish parliament. All the old Irish anti-union laws remained in force until the general repeal of the combination laws in 1824.

Before the repeal of Wilberforce's act, parliament appointed a select committee to inquire into three things, viz., the export of machinery, the emigration of skilled craftsmen, and the laws against trade unions. Francis Place, though not a member of parliament himself, had a considerable influence on parliament and was an adroit political tactician. By working through certain Radical MPs with whom he was friendly he managed to get the select committee packed with members who were not particularly hostile to the trade unions.

The committee travelled to many parts of the United Kingdom. It received evidence from employers, trade unionists, magistrates, policemen and from other interested people. Its report, as W. P. Ryan acknowledges in *The Irish Labour Movement,* is one of the main sources of information about the early Irish trade unions.

For example, Patrick Farrell, secretary of the Regular Carpenters of Dublin, told the committee that his union had between 400 and 500 members and that in the city of Dublin there were another 300 carpenters who were not union members.

Farrell also stated that the union was controlled by a council of five elected leaders whose meeting places were known to the police. The employers, according to Farrell, more or less accepted the union, recognised it and often sent their foremen to the Council of Five when they needed workmen.

But all the employers were not just so friendly. Edward Carolan, a master carpenter and a former member of the union, told the select committee that the Council of Five had once organised an attack on his workshop because he was employing non-union men. Carolan described how he repulsed this attack and how he was forced to open fire on the union carpenters. During the struggle a man by the name of McDonnell, a union member, was fatally wounded.

The authorities took no action against Carolan, whereupon the union, on the advice of its solicitor, William Hall, instigated a prosecution against Carolan, who was eventually brought to trial, but was acquitted.

Hall was an early labour lawyer and was well known in Dublin trade union circles. He had been acting on behalf of the unions since 1808 and was often called upon to mediate in disputes between the unions and the employers. He told the select committee that in his opinion the law against trade unions in Ireland was more severe than the law in England. He said he had seen men whipped in Dublin for simple contraventions of the combination laws, yet these men had been guilty of no violence.

Michael Farrell, chief constable of the Dublin police, told the committee that every one of the sixteen trades in the city had its own club or trade union. He had no evidence, however, of the unions being joined in one federation, though he did think they helped one another with money during strikes and especially if the trouble arose out of the employment of non-union workmen.

Another witness, Jeremiah Houghton, an employer in the woollen trade, said that all the workmen belonged to one union and that this union was run by a secret committee that met around a table covered with green cloth. Houghton said that the committee terrorised industry, summoned union members if they violated the rules, and often fined them as much as twenty shillings.

The Board of Green Cloth is something of a legend in Irish trade union history, even to the present day. John Swift in his *History of the Dublin Bakers* has stated that:

... the term "going before the Green Cloth" is still used in the Dublin Bakers' Union when a member is summoned to appear before the committee.

Sidney and Beatrice Webb were both convinced that there was a committee such as Houghton described and that its control explained why the Dublin trade unions were the best organised in the Kingdom. In their history they have written that the Dublin unions:

... ruthlessly enforced their by-laws for the regulation of their respective industries and formed a committee, the so-called Board of Green Cloth, whose dictates became the terror of the employers.

W. P. Ryan describes, in ironic language, how the board must have appeared to the Dublin employers:

... the fateful board was clothed with a more sinister green decade after decade. It was the centre not only of the woollen conspirators but of all trade unionism. The plotters, the terrorists from all trades, who sat around in the watches of the night were no longer satisfied with the simple fines of up to a sovereign that seemed bad enough to Mr. Houghton. They were out for spoil and rapine and blood. They made tyrannous rules, decided on iniquitous demands, and planned the laying low of unoffending 'colts' (i.e. non-unionists) and masters. And murderous men, with eyes as red as the cloth on the board was green, were ever ready at hand, thirsting to carry out their right devilish behests.

According to the reports of magistrates and Castle officials the Dublin trade unions in the 1820s were militant to the point of violence and terror.

In September 1824 a gang of Dublin carpenters beat up an employer, in his own home, because he refused to dismiss a non-union workman. A few weeks later twenty plasterers attacked a man who worked for less than the trade union rate of pay. In October a carpenter died after he, along with another man, had been beaten for ignoring union rules.

And the violence continued. In November, Dublin Castle informed Sir Robert Peel, who was then Home Secretary, that within the previous month

. . . no less than four men have been killed or have had their skulls fractured for violating the laws of their union.

Early in January 1825 it was reported that employers in the construction industry, in coach-building and in the clothing trade were being attacked by their workmen. One master builder had to seek police protection because he feared the unions were planning to wreck his house.

In July that year a blacksmith had his skull fractured when he refused to join in a strike, a painter was beaten by union men, an apprentice shipwright was murdered out at Ringsend and his companion very seriously injured.

There were riots in the Liberties of Dublin when the women in the silk-weaving trade went on strike. At Kilkenny, union men surrounded Pickering's paper-mill when the management brought in strike-breakers from Scotland.

In 1826 Dublin experienced what was undoubtedly the first general strike in Irish history. It was a strike about prices, inflation and the value of Irish money. Bread was scarce in the city that year and very expensive. Moreover, bad coins, counterfeits and even worthless tokens were often passed for money. Many employers took advantage of the circulation of this dross and paid their workers in coins that were worthless.

Irish money was inferior in value to English money and, by law, thirteen Irish pence were equal to one English shilling. Yet many shopkeepers and traders, contrary to the law, refused to pay more than twelve Irish pence for an English shilling.

All this gave rise to mass discontent which brought the workers in many trades on to the streets in protest. The employers, led by the Duke of Leinster and Sheriff Mallett, retaliated by declaring a lock-out. This led to further violence in the city.

During the 1820s many trade unionists were arrested and accused of murder, riot and assault. It was the trials of these men that brought Daniel O'Connell into contact with the unions. As an attorney he defended trade unionists when they appeared

in court. He also became acquainted with the ways in which
the trade unions operated and was later to use his knowledge
against the unions.

4

MORE NORTHERN PIONEERS

ONE of the labour leaders caught up in Francis Place's
campaign for repeal of the combination laws was John Doherty,
secretary of the cotton-spinners' union in Manchester. Doherty,
whom Place disliked and more than once described as 'a stubborn
hot-headed Roman Catholic,' was born in Buncrana, Co.
Donegal in 1799.

Between 1814 and 1817 he worked as a cotton-spinner in
Larne. From there he emigrated to Manchester where he soon
got involved in the cotton-spinners' underground union. He
led a big strike in 1819, was arrested, convicted and imprisoned
in Lancaster Castle for two years.

At that time, which was nearly thirty years before the Great
Famine, Manchester was packed with Irish immigrants. In their
book, *The Town Labourer*, which describes some of the conditions under which people lived and worked during the Industrial Revolution, J. L. and Barbara Hammond have written:

A great number of the emigrants came from Ireland. During the
riots against power-looms in 1826 there were said to be as many as
30,000 or 40,000 Irish weavers in Manchester alone. The Poor Law
Commissioners' Report of 1822 contains a graphic picture of the
destitute Irish families arriving at Liverpool to seek employment in
the manufacturing districts.

By 1841 there were more than 400,000 Irish-born people in
Britain; ten years later, in 1851, the number of Irish-born
residents was 700,000. To this number should be added a
perhaps greater number of second-generation Irish who were
born in England but whose outlook was as markedly Irish as
the outlook of their parents.

The Irish in Britain remained passionately interested in the
plight of the land they had left, because most of them had families and friends still in their home country. Yet they were also
deeply involved in the problems of industrial Britain. They
usually made for the centres of industry, the towns of Lancashire
especially, where they took the lowest-paid jobs, being weavers,
general labourers, porters and navvies.

In 1841 the County of Lancashire had more than 100,000 Irish-born inhabitants, of whom 50,000 were in Liverpool and 30,000 in Manchester. Nearly half of Scotland's 100,000 Irish immigrants lived in Glasgow.

Frederick Engels, communist and cotton-manufacturer, writing on the *Condition of the Working Class in England, in 1844,* saw these Irish immigrants as low-wage labour with whom the English workers had to compete. Irish families, living at abysmally low levels in slum cellars, alleyways and enclosed courts, forced down the wages of the English—at least according to Engels. He has described how some of the Irish lived in a district of Manchester, 'Little Ireland' with which he was familiar, and where he saw:

. . . the inhabitants in dilapidated cottages, the windows of which are broken and patched with oilskin. The doors and the posts are rotten and broken. . . . The worst dwellings were good enough for them. Their clothing causes them little trouble so long as it holds together by a single thread. Shoes they know not. Their food consists of potatoes and potatoes only. Whatever they earn beyond their needs they spend on drink. What does such a race want with high wages?

That was how Frederick Engels saw the poorest Irish in England, and no doubt his description was neither exaggerated nor untrue. But many of the English poor lived in similar conditions. Moreover, it was often alleged that the Irish in Britain, far from being cheap labourers, were among the foremost militants in the trade union movement.

Peter Ewart, a textile manufacturer who gave evidence to a commission which was set up to inquire into the *State of the Irish Poor in Great Britain,* in 1836, said that:

. . . wherever there is discontent or a disposition to combine, or turnouts among workpeople, the Irish are leaders; they are the most difficult to reason with and convince on the subject of wages and regulations in factories.

Several other textile manufacturers in the North of England were of the opinion that the Irish took a leading part in most advanced movements of discontent and did not refrain from intimidation and violence in order to enforce solidarity among the workers.

A Catholic priest who lived in Manchester during the 1830s said that:

. . . the Irish were prone to take part in trade unions and secret societies more than the English.

John Doherty was the first Irishman to become a leader in the British trade union movement, though he and Francis Place held radically different views on the future of the unions. Place was convinced that repeal of the combination laws would take the militancy out of trade unionism. Being no longer illegal, the unions, he thought, would feel less aggrieved and would, therefore, be less inclined to go on strike. Francis Burdett, one of the MPs who supported Place, believed that after repeal the unions would no longer be needed and would gradually disappear.

Doherty thought otherwise. To him the unions had a great future, but they were still not well enough organised to exert the influence they were capable of exerting. Trade unions, he suggested, should be nation-wide and in every trade and industry.

Putting this theory into practice in 1829, Doherty organised a conference of Irish, Scottish and English cotton-workers and from that conference launched the Grand General Union of Cotton Spinners of Great Britain and Ireland. This was the first of the national, as distinct from the merely local, unions.

Having formed a national union Doherty next made plans for a federation of all the unions and, in 1830, inspired a conference that gave rise to the National Association for the Protection of Labour—the first trades union congress. Doherty was elected general secretary of the National Association.

The association was a federation of twenty unions from several different industries and within a few months its affiliations had grown to 150 unions. These unions represented about 20,000 workers in textiles, engineering, shipbuilding, coalmining, building, potteries and furniture manufacture. The trade unions in Belfast were affiliated.

But despite its promising beginnings the National Association failed. In the first place Doherty had difficulty in getting the support of the influential London unions. Then his colleagues on the executive committee of the association quarrelled with him. They thought him too ambitious and disliked his proposal to move the headquarters to London and to start a newspaper.

Doherty was a pioneer in Labour journalism. His first newspaper, which appeared in 1828, was *The Conciliator*, but like most working-class publications it did not last for very long. In 1831 he became editor of *The Voice of the People* which was, surprisingly, equal to the *Manchester Guardian* in size and layout, professionally designed and fairly well supported by advertisers.

The Voice of the People denounced landlordism in Ireland. It condemned the revival of Orangeism in Ulster during the

1830s. It exposed the truck system whereby many unscrupulous employers often defrauded their employees. It organised public meetings in support of trade unionism, the extension of the parliamentary franchise to the working class, and factory reform.

After his quarrel with the executive committee of the National Association, Doherty gave up his job as general secretary and seems, consequently, to have lost interest in the trade unions. But he continued, until his death in 1854, to agitate for factory reform and against the employment of children in industry.

Although the combination laws were repealed in 1824, many magistrates continued to persecute and punish trade unionists with great severity. The case of the Tolpuddle Martyrs, in 1834, is one of the most important events in trade union history. The men concerned were six farm labourers in the village of Tolpuddle in Dorset. They formed a trade union, in order to raise their wages from seven shillings a week to ten shillings, and were promptly arrested and brought before the local magistrates on a charge of conspiracy and of administering illegal oaths. They were found guilty and sent to the convict settlements in Australia. Their conviction caused a national outcry in which George Kerr, a cabinetmaker in Belfast, was to be involved. (See Appendix I).

Kerr was chairman at a meeting called by the Belfast unions to protest against the Tolpuddle sentences. This publicised him as a leading trade unionist and he was consequently asked by the cabinetmakers of Derry City to advise them about forming a union. The Derry men had been under attack from their employers and had had their wages cut by as much as one-third. Kerr offered to visit Derry and help them form a branch of the cabinetmakers' union. But from the moment he entered the city of Derry he was followed by the employers' spies. After he left, having held a meeting and formed a union branch, two of the local cabinetmakers were arrested on the orders of Joshua Gillespie, Mayor of Derry, and charged with administering illegal oaths.

At the same time Gillespie issued a warrant for the arrest of Kerr, who was taken in Belfast two days later and brought back to Derry for questioning. Kerr afterwards wrote an account of his experiences at the hands of the Derry magistrates and had it published in Belfast under the title *Exposition of Legislative Tyranny and Defence of the Trade Unions*. In this pamphlet he had described how Gillespie held him in custody and made his release impossible by imposing a sum of bail that he could not, by the remotest chance, have raised. He was taken to jail,

forced to put on prison clothes and locked in a cell over which
was written 'committed to the assizes.'

The assizes were due to be held the following July, so Kerr
faced the prospect of spending at least six months in prison.
He wrote to Dublin Castle asking to be released on bail and
was told to put his application to the Court of King's Bench.
Perhaps he did this. He was released, though in his pamphlet
he did not say how.

The case ended when the Grand Jury ignored the bill of
indictment against him and his companions. There was, in fact,
no case to try. Gillespie and his henchmen were guilty of unlawful arrest, but no action was ever taken against them.

During the 1830s William Dalzell Finlay, editor and proprietor of the *Northern Whig*, a radical newspaper published in
Belfast, found himself in what seemed almost endless conflict
with his journeymen printers, all of whom were members of the
Belfast Typographical Society. He tried to break this union, in
1834, by bringing men in from Scotland. He did this at considerable personal expense, travelling to Glasgow and Edinburgh
in search of suitable recruits. When he got the men he wanted
he paid their fares and expenses back to Belfast.

But Finlay's journeymen had little difficulty in upsetting these
plans. They followed him to Scotland, met the workmen whom
he recruited and persuaded them not to take up employment
on the *Northern Whig*. This was not really difficult because the
Belfast printers, like their colleagues in Dublin, had contacts
all over Britain. The typographical societies on both sides of
the Irish Sea had been in association since as early as 1800.
They helped one another financially during strikes. Any union
printer travelling in search of work was entitled to the assistance
of the local society wherever he went.

Union loyalty among the compositors was so strong that when
Finlay's Scottish recruits learned why he was offering them
employment and paying their expenses they did not hesitate
to break their contracts with him, even though by doing so they
ran the risk of being sent to prison.

Frustrated in Scotland, Finlay turned to Dublin but there
he found the local union, the Dublin Typographical Society,
determined to stand by the men of the *Northern Whig*. Nonetheless he persuaded some Dublin printers to return to Belfast
with him. A few years later, in 1838, when he gave evidence to
the parliamentary committee that was inquiring into trade
unionism, he told what happened when he and the Dubliners
reached Belfast.

A crowd of at least 2,000 people were waiting for them at the Belfast coach terminal and followed them to the office of the *Northern Whig*. The situation was serious enough for Finlay to seek police protection, to arm himself with a sword-stick, and to issue guns to the Dublin men. He afterwards prosecuted two of the Belfast union men for threats and intimidation and had them sent to prison.

Finlay believed that with the Dublin men now in his employment he had broken the union and this encouraged him to engage other non-union men from outside Belfast. Yet within a year or so he found that all these workmen had joined the union and he was again faced with demands for higher wages and better working conditions. He had to concede a reduction in the number of apprentices and to raise the wages of journeymen to twenty-five shillings a week.

But W. D. Finlay was not easily defeated. He challenged the union again, in 1838, when he hired pauper boys and trained them secretly in the backrooms of his printing works. When the printers went on strike, over the case of a journalist on the staff being asked to set type, he had these boys at hand to run the press.

And he afterwards claimed that with these children, the energetic help of his good wife, and the unpaid labour of some local gentlemen, he had put down the union. He advised other employers to use the same methods. In fact he told the 1838 committee that he and other employers had agreed among themselves to fight the unions—but he was clever enough not to put this agreement in writing.

Finlay was, of course, quite mistaken. He could not suppress the trade unions. The Belfast Typographical Society, with which he fought such bitter battles, continued and is today merged in the National Graphical Association, a union with members throughout Britain and in all parts of Ireland except Dublin where the Dublin Typographical and Provident Society is still the dominant union in the city's printing and newspaper industries.

The Dublin Typographical Society is one of the oldest trade unions in Ireland. In the early years of the nineteenth century its members received benefit payments when they were unemployed, travelling allowances when they went outside Dublin in search of employment, strike pay and funeral benefit. They were also entitled to grants of £4 each if they emigrated to England and £8 if they went to the United States of America.

Thomas Daly, secretary of this union, gave evidence to the

1838 committee. He said that representatives of the compositors in each of the printing firms and newspapers met in a Dublin public house every Saturday night to discuss union business. The membership of the union then consisted of 260 journeymen and 180 apprentices. Daly's salary as secretary was twenty guineas a year.

In 1836 the Irish typographical societies set up a national federation, which they called the Irish Typographical Union and, in 1844, this federation joined with the unions in England and Scotland to form the National Typographical Association. The National Typographical Association broke up in 1848 and when it was reorganised as the Provincial Typographical Association the following year the Irish societies did not join. Those were the years of the Great Famine when many organisations, including the trade unions, were wrecked and dislocated.

The secretary of the Irish Typographical Union was Matthew Ryan, a Dublin compositor. He told the 1838 committee that the union had subscribed £100 to the Belfast Typographical Society to help them in the struggle against Finlay. The union also sent £90 to the printers of Newry when they were in dispute with James Henderson, proprietor of the *Newry Commercial Telegraph*. Henderson afterwards claimed that his men acted on orders from Dublin. They put forward what he described as 'stern demands'—a minimum wage of twenty-five shillings a week, a ten-hour day and not more than four apprentices. He resisted these demands, and when the men went on strike he tried, like Finlay, to bring in replacements from Scotland. The Scotsmen got as far as Newry, but Henderson never saw them. They were persuaded—by bribes, he alleged—to go back home.

The idea of a national federation of all the Irish typographical societies came up again in 1863. It was put forward by the Dublin union but none of the other local societies were, it seems, interested. So for the time being the concept of one trade union for all printers in Ireland was forgotten.

J. D. Clarkson gives an interesting account of the rules under which young journeymen compositors were admitted to the Dublin society in the early years of the nineteenth century:

... as soon as a Dublin apprentice terminates his term, he is proposed by one person as a fit person to become a member of the society and his indentures are handed in; he then remains upon the book of the society until his name goes round all the different printing establishments in Dublin, to know if he is a person of good character and qualified to be admitted. If the majority are in favour he comes forward and pays a guinea, and then every week he is employed he pays sixpence towards the expenses of the society.

If the candidate for membership had served his apprenticeship outside Dublin he had to pay two guineas entrance fee, provided, of course, that he was accepted into membership. If he were already a member of another typographical society the entrance fee was reduced to seventeen shillings and sixpence.

Philip Dixon Hardy, publisher of the *Dublin Penny Journal*, was another of the master printers who gave evidence to the 1838 committee. He complained that the Dublin society had insisted on a minimum wage of thirty shillings a week for journeymen, and "expected to be paid as much for a page containing woodcuts as if they had set the page entirely." He also said that the union firmly refused to work with non-union men, and imposed a strict limitation on the number of apprentices entering the trade.

In limiting apprenticeships the Dublin society was merely carrying out the rules of the Irish Typographical Union. These rules stated that there should be only one apprentice in a print-shop with two journeymen, two apprentices with four journeymen, three apprentices with six journeymen, and where more than six journeymen were employed the number of apprentices was not to exceed four.

The employers sometimes admitted that the unions had good reason for insisting on the control of apprenticeships. P. D. Hardy himself said that "many printing offices in Ireland were conducted entirely without journeymen." The young men trained in such places were generally incompetent compositors, yet they would come to Dublin and claim to have served seven years and to be competent craftsmen. Hardy agreed that when a man was properly trained in the business and educated he should "not be expected to hunt the world for employment."

Henderson of Newry thought that two apprentices at four shillings a week each "were equal in labour power" to one journeyman at twenty-five shillings, but even he agreed that it was not entirely wise to have too many apprentices. Being boys they could be careless and even deliberately destructive at times.

Michael Staunton, proprietor of the two Dublin newspapers, the *Morning Register* and the *Weekly Register*, and also one of the most impressive witnesses to appear before the committee, estimated that one apprentice to every three journeymen should be enough to supply the labour needs of the printing trade in Dublin. He believed that throughout the whole of Ireland the number of apprentices in printing probably exceeded the number of journeymen.

The conditions under which apprentices entered the trade, Hardy said, varied from firm to firm. He himself asked parents for a premium of £20 and made them responsible for the boy's board and lodgings during the first two years of training. In the third year he paid the apprentice five shillings a week, with annual increases that brought the wages up to ten shillings a week in the seventh and last year.

Henderson asked for no premium but expected parents to pay for their son's board and lodgings. The wages he paid his apprentices were about twenty per cent less than what Hardy paid.

Among the notable disputes in the printing trade in those times was a strike on the *Carrick Morning Post* whose proprietor, Richard Lonergan, in 1825, tried to dilute the trade with apprentices. Lonergan refused to negotiate with his journeymen and there was, consequently, a walk-out. The upshot of this dispute was that Lonergan and some non-union men whom he engaged were waylaid and attacked by the strikers, seven of whom were eventually prosecuted and bound over to keep the peace.

A trade dispute seems to have been one of the reasons—or perhaps one of the excuses—for closing down the *Dublin Courier,* a pro-Castle newspaper, in 1825. The staff of this paper went on strike because they could get no money—they actually said they could not even get their due wages—from what they called 'a bungling and imbecile management.' The management retaliated by accusing the journeymen of political bias, a suggestion which the union thought ridiculous, because the men on strike said it made no difference to them what politics the newspaper followed, provided they were paid for the work they did—and paid properly.

5

O'CONNELL AND THE IRISH CHARTISTS

IN 1832 the Westminster parliament passed a reform act which extended the vote to the middle classes of the industrial towns but not to the workers. This exclusion of the workers from the franchise along with widespread opposition to the New Poor Law of 1834 gave rise to Chartism, a movement which demanded civil rights for everyone. Chartism took its name from *The People's Charter*, a document which set out six points:

Universal manhood suffrage,
Abolition of property qualifications for members of parliament,
Secret ballots in all elections,
Equal electoral divisions,
Salaries for members of parliament,
Annual general elections.

All these points of the Charter, except annual general elections, were conceded one after another, between the Reform Act of 1867, which did give the vote to the workers, and the Parliament Act of 1911. But in the 1830s, when the Chartists roused the whole of England in support of them, they were regarded as revolutionary demands. Had they been conceded then they would have benefited the Irish in the same way as they would have benefited the English because Ireland was then part of the United Kingdom.

Yet Ireland's trade unionists, apart from a few men in Belfast, Dublin and in one or two other places, did not join the Chartist agitation. The Irish unions, especially those in the southern provinces, supported the Repeal movement—Repeal of the 1800 Act of Union—and trusted Daniel O'Connell when he assured them that the re-establishment of a parliament and government in Ireland would protect native industry, promote employment and increase wages.

In the autumn of 1832 the carpenters of Dublin, along with several other unions, published resolutions in support of Repeal and sent petitions to Westminster. Similar resolutions were passed by the unions in Cork and Tullamore. Their main argument was that the Legislative Union with Britain had caused the decline of Irish industry and trade.

The unions in Cork had so much influence in the Repeal movement that, it was said, they were able to defeat the parliamentary nominees of the aristocratic Boyles and Hutchinsons in the 1833 general election. They persuaded nearly all the local Liberals to follow O'Connell. Under their influence Cork presented a united front in favour of Repeal.

The Conservatives in Dublin denounced these Repeal activities and through their newspaper, the *Dublin Evening Post*, advised the unions not to be embroiled in politics, to leave public affairs to those best fitted by education and class to legislate wisely, and to confine their activities to matters that concerned the wages and employment of workpeople.

The unions ignored the advice of the *Dublin Evening Post* and proceeded to support their resolutions by organising a Repeal demonstration in Dublin. This was to take the form of a march right through the city to O'Connell's house in Merrion Square; but when Dublin Castle banned the march O'Connell advised the unions to obey the ban.

It took the Irish trade unions a long time to realise that O'Connell, far from being their well-beloved leader, was one of their bitterest enemies. In 1838, when the Westminster parliament was discussing the case of five Scottish cotton-workers who had been transported for forming a trade union, he said:

... there is no tyranny equal to that exercised by the trade unionists in Dublin over their fellow labourers.

He went on to accuse the unions, in a long and closely-argued speech, of ruining many factories and trades in Dublin, Bandon, Belfast and elsewhere, and of undermining the shipbuilding industry with their endless demands for higher wages. At the end of the debate, on O'Connell's suggestion, parliament appointed a committee to inquire into trade unions. This was the committee to which Finlay, Staunton, Hardy, Daly and the others gave evidence. O'Connell was one of its members.

In 1835 O'Connell and his party of Irish MPs formed an alliance with the English Whig Free Traders, then in power, and supported them against the reformers and Chartists on three of the most controversial issues of the day, viz. the 'New Poor Law,' the trade unions, and factory legislation.

The 'New Poor Law,' the 1834 act, denied outdoor relief to the able-bodied unemployed and drove thousands of poor people into the 'union workhouses.' Conditions in the work-houses, as the Poor Law Commissioners had decreed, were almost as bad as in the prisons and worse than the worst possible conditions of unemployment in the factories and mines. Discipline in the workhouses was rigid and often cruel. Inmates were flogged for petty theft and locked up for such crimes as giving away their meals, refusing to work, or going into town without permission. This was all part of the *laissez faire,* or free-for-all, economy in which O'Connell and the Whigs so firmly believed.

O'Connell and the Whigs denounced the trade unions as conspiracies which were formed to restrict the employers' right to run industry as they thought best.

For the same reasons they were against factory reform. No parliament, in their view, had any right to pass laws that would regulate working conditions in the coal-mines, the cotton-mills or other workplaces. Such laws, they argued, would be undue and unwise interference with the rights of private property.

O'Connell upheld this doctrine. In June 1838 when Lord Ashley, the pioneer of factory legislation, proposed a bill which he believed would have improved the Factories Act of 1833 and "more effectively regulate factory works" O'Connell defended the interests of the employers. He advised parliament "not to be guilty of the childish folly of regulating the labour of adults." He castigated Ashley and the other reformers for what he called "their ridiculous humanity." They would end, he said, "by converting the manufacturers into beggars."

Despite his antipathy to trade unionism and his hatred of factory reform, O'Connell was regarded as a liberal and a radical in politics. Presumably he should then have agreed with the six points of *The People's Charter*. Yet he was persistently hostile to Chartism and when he faced a charge of conspiracy, in 1844, his defence was that he had saved Ireland from Chartism. He denounced the Chartists before a Dublin jury packed with Orangemen:

... you have seen my conduct with respect to the Chartists. They were up in arms, up in insurrection through England, crowding in tens of thousands through all her manufacturing towns. Their doctrines were spreading, their disciples increasing, for there was something fascinating for the poorer classes in the principles of the Charter. It purposed a violation of all property. Its followers were numerous. They offered me aid. I denounced them. I denounced their doctrines. I drove them from Ireland. It has been read to you that the moment we discovered that a Chartist had joined our association his money was returned to him and his name struck off the list of members.

O'Connell ended his speech by declaring that if he had not opposed Chartism "it would have passed over and spread from one end of Ireland to the other." "I shall ever rejoice," he said, "that I kept Ireland free from this pollution."

In the same speech and in equally virulent language he denounced the trade unions:

... you must all remember what a frightful combination existed eight years ago among the workmen and operatives of Dublin. Lives were lost in the public streets. Men were assaulted with brutal violence. The combination had spread to such a frightful extent that the public authorities were unable to cope with it. I came forward. I opposed the combination single-handed at the risk not only of my popularity but of my very existence. At the meeting in the Exchange the operatives were infuriated against me and I owed the preservation of my life to the police. I persevered, persuaded those that were most ferocious against me, and from that day to this not a single combination outrage has occurred in Dublin.

This was O'Connell's defence. In London *The Times* commented that "there was something pathetic in the spectacle of this septuagenarian Irishman, arraigned on an absurd charge, apologising for his whole career to a packed jury and a bench of placemen."

Chartism first appeared in Ireland in 1839 when a trade union group in Dublin asked the Chartist Convention, then meeting in Birmingham, to send a speaker who would explain the six points to an Irish audience. The Convention sent Robert Lowery, a Newcastle-upon-Tyne tailor who had spent many years at sea. Lowery was a militant who would not have ruled out physical force as one way of getting reforms. It was arranged that he should speak at a meeting in the London Tavern which was in Henry Street, Dublin.

When the O'Connellites learned of this meeting they organised a party to wreck it. They invaded the London Tavern, prevented Lowery from speaking and denounced Chartism as a revolutionary movement that would lead the people of Ireland into violent and illegal activities. Eventually the meeting broke up in confusion. Lowery and his companions fled through the back door of the tavern to escape injury. Later O'Connell commended his followers for what he called their 'loyal demonstration.'

Despite attacks like the one in the London Tavern and the hostility of the O'Connellites, the Irish Chartists continued to hold meetings and to distribute copies of the Charter and of the Chartist newspaper, the *Northern Star*. There were Chartist groups in Belfast as well as in Dublin, in Newry, Drogheda and even as far away as Sligo town and Loughrea in County Galway.

Most of these Irish Chartists were working men, rural labourers or small farmers, though one Catholic priest, Fr. Patrick Ryan of Donabate, near Dublin, and a Dublin merchant named Patrick O'Higgins were prominent in the movement. In August 1841 the Irish Chartists formed the Irish Universal Suffrage Association of which O'Higgins was elected president.

The association was denounced by the Catholic clergy, spied upon by the police and physically attacked by the O'Connellites, but it continued to hold meetings and to circulate Chartist propaganda.

In 1842 the association published *Chartism and Repeal*. This was a pamphlet which called for an alliance of English Chartists and Irish Repealers. Another pamphlet, *Civil and Religious Liberty*, alleged that Irish Chartists were being refused the sacraments by some Catholic priests.

The Chartist agitation continued in Ireland until 1848 when O'Higgins was arrested, on a charge of hoarding weapons, and kept in prison without trial for nearly nine months. He was released unconditionally after a public protest.

In England the acknowledged leader of the Chartists was Fergus O'Connor, a Corkman who, during the 1830s, had been one of O'Connell's Irish Party in the Westminster parliament. He was elected for Cork County in 1833 but soon found that he could not agree with O'Connell and the Whigs on such issues as trade unionism, factory legislation and the poor law. He was unseated by petition in 1835, either through connivance of his enemies or because he genuinely did not possess the necessary property qualifications, as the petitioners alleged, to sit as a county member. After leaving parliament he turned to agitation among the working class and became editor of the *Northern Star*, a newspaper which had a wide and influential circulation in the industrial towns. Through it O'Connor became known as a working-class leader. He addressed rallies of working people in Bradford, Birmingham, Manchester and on the Yorkshire moors. He advocated armed rebellion in support of the Charter. He organised political strikes and led demonstrations and marches to Westminster.

For these activities O'Connor was imprisoned, along with other Chartist leaders, and threatened with transportation. But despite the hostility of magistrates and the ridicule of politicians and political writers he led the Chartist movement until its decline in the late 1840s.

In 1847 he entered parliament again, this time as member for Nottingham, but soon after his election he went mad, assaulted another member in the House and had to be taken away. He died in 1855 and his funeral was one of the largest ever seen in England; more than 50,000 people followed the hearse across Kennington Common.

The British working class never had another leader like Fergus O'Connor. His indignation at the conditions under which people had to work in the factories and mines and to live in the slums of the industrial towns was profound. He felt deeply for the starving Irish farmers and landless labourers, for the emaciated handicraftsmen made redundant by the Industrial Revolution, and for the paupers doomed to live within the hated workhouses. He often said:

... our movement is a Labour movement originated in the first instance by the fustian jackets, the blistered hands and the unshorn chins.

O'Connor, whose forebears were aristocrats and revolutionaries, was an Irish Nationalist who believed, like O'Connell, that the Act of Union should have been repealed and Ireland's parliament restored. But, unlike O'Connell, he could see that Ireland's enemies, the Whig and Tory politicians, the landlords and factory-owners of England, were also the enemies of the British working people. He tirelessly urged, therefore, that there should be an alliance of Chartists and Repealers against the English ruling classes. O'Connell, banker, brewer and landlord that he himself was, feared such an alliance. He and his followers denounced O'Connor as "a violent and disgraced Irishman." They directed much of their activities towards undermining his influence in Britain and in Ireland.

6

BRITISH TRADE UNIONS IN IRELAND

By 1850, after nearly a century of technical progress, Britain had become the world's most important industrial country—the workshop of the world. The achievements of British industrial capitalism were put on display at the Great Exhibition which was held in the Crystal Palace, London in 1851. The future looked good. The British nation was optimistic.

The British working class, especially those who had the good fortune to be skilled craftsmen, responded to this optimism by forming 'new model' trade unions. They adopted the motto *Defence not Defiance* because they had no wish to quarrel unnecessarily with their employers. All they asked was recognition for their trade unions and some share of the national prosperity.

The leaders of the new model unions, men like William Allen and William Newton of the Amalgamated Society of Engineers, and like Robert Applegarth of the Amalgamated Society of Carpenters and Joiners were not socialists. They were followers of the Liberal Party. Some were Conservatives—or at least believed themselves to be so. To these men the old revolutionary leaders of the 1820s and '30s—Robert Owen, Fergus O'Connor, John Doherty, the Chartists—were irrelevant and outdated.

They lived in the age of expanding Imperial power, the golden years of the British Empire.

Chartism was dying as the new model unions were born. Applegarth, Allen, Newton and their followers wanted to hear nothing about "fustian jackets, blistered hands and unshorn chins." They represented skilled men, the aristocrats of labour in mid-Victorian Britain.

The unions they led restricted membership to properly-qualified, apprentice-trained craftsmen and, reflecting the class snobbery of the nineteenth-century English artisan, ignored the great mass of unskilled labourers.

Not only did they disregard the unskilled, the thought of organising women workers, of whom hundreds of thousands worked in slave conditions throughout the United Kingdom, never crossed their minds.

It was not until the 1880s when socialism was revived in the British Labour movement that the first effective unions for unskilled men and for women workers were formed. And it was not until the year 1944, in the middle of the Second World War, that the Amalgamated Engineering Union (successor of the ASE) relaxed its all-male rule and allowed women engineering workers to become members.

In Ireland there were several unions of unskilled workers, general labourers and dockers as early as the 1860s. The Limerick dock labourers had a union in 1860. In 1875 the Dublin Quay Labourers' Union, with 1,500 members, took part in the O'Connell centenary celebrations. During the last twenty-five years of the nineteenth century several unions were formed for the Irish labourers. Some of these unions failed, others remained and eventually merged with larger cross-Channel unions.

The Amalgamated Society of Engineers (now the Amalgamated Union of Engineering and Foundry Workers) was the first of the new model unions. In the year of its formation, 1851, it had five branches in Ireland. These were in Dublin, Belfast, Cork, Drogheda and Derry, though most of the members were in the Dublin and Belfast branches.

By 1858 branches of the ASE had been set up in Dundalk, Limerick, Newry, Lisburn and Waterford, and by 1868 the membership of this union in Ireland had reached 1,300. Today the AEF has more than 30,000 members in Ireland, most of them in the North where there are many old-established as well as recently-formed engineering firms. The total membership of the AEF in Britain, Ireland and abroad is more than 1,250,000. It is one of the largest trade unions in the world.

The original Irish branches of the ASE marked the beginning of what are known as the 'amalgamated' or 'British-based' unions in Ireland. Amalgamated unions of lithographic printers, boilermakers, carpenters and joiners, cabinetmakers, bricklayers and craftsmen of many kinds set up branches in Ireland during the second half of the nineteenth century, between 1851 and 1900.

Often—for example, in the case of the Amalgamated Society of Carpenters and Joiners—these British unions competed with the older Irish unions for members. The Amalgamated Society of Carpenters and Joiners was established in 1860; it came into Ireland in 1866 and for nearly thirty years competed in Dublin with the Regular Carpenters, and in Cork with the Ancient Corporation of Carpenters.

The Regular Carpenters held out against this competition. In 1890 they had 600 members while the British union had only 120, but in that year, during a campaign for reduction in the working week, the Dublin union voluntarily agreed to merge with the British union. Through this merger membership of the carpenters' union in Dublin soon increased to more than 1,000.

Three years later, in 1893, the Ancient Corporation of Carpenters in Cork joined the amalgamated society. By that time the older union had 200 members in the city, while the British union had never been able to increase its membership above twenty.

These mergers were really to the advantage of the British union. Both the Regular Carpenters of Dublin and the Ancient Corporation of Carpenters owned valuable property which was transferred to the amalgamated society when the unions merged.

Through time the question of whether trade unions in Ireland should be exclusively Irish organisations, Irish-based and controlled, or branches of British unions, became a matter of serious and prolonged controversy. It was so in 1920, for example, when the attitude of the British Labour Party and the British TUC to Ireland's fight for political independence was dubious and when some branches of British unions in Ireland broke away to form separate Irish unions. It was mentioned at a conference of the Communist International in 1919 by two anonymous Irish delegates, 'Comrade X' and 'Comrade Y.' It arose again in 1944 when some of the Irish unions broke away from the Irish Trades Union Congress to form a new body, the Congress of Irish Unions. And the fact that there were Irish unions and British unions operating in Ireland led to important developments in Irish trade union law in 1941.

Today, because of history, politics and economic development, British unions are numerically strong in Northern Ireland; they represent about eight out of every ten organised workers in that part of the country. The Irish unions are correspondingly strong in the Republic of Ireland.

Trades councils began to be formed in Ireland from the early 1860s. In 1863 thirty unions in Dublin set up the United Trades Association, which was, in fact, a trades council for the city. The following year these unions proposed that there should be a federation of all the trade unions in Ireland—an Irish TUC.

This federation was in the process of being formed when, in 1868, the Trades Union Congress appeared in Britain. With the rise of the British TUC many union members in Ireland, especially those who were in the amalgamated unions, turned to London for leadership. They did not then realise, and it took them a long time to find out, that trade union leaders in Britain are seldom interested in Irish affairs and indeed do not always want to understand the problems of the trade unions in this country.

This became evident in 1880 when the British TUC met in Dublin. At that meeting those English delegates who spoke revealed that they knew little about the political and industrial problems of Ireland and nothing about the history and traditions of Irish trade unionism. They did not know that John Doherty and Fergus O'Connor and thousands of other Irishmen had pioneered trade unionism and socialism in England.

Clarkson in *Labour and Nationalism in Ireland* suggests that when meeting in Dublin the leaders of the TUC may have thought they "were venturing on a bold exploit" comparable to the adventures of their empire-building countrymen then exploring the jungles and forests of Africa.

And it seemed, judging from the tone of their speeches, that those stout English trade unionists were surprised to find "their Irish brethren had not brought their pigs and shillelaghs to the conference." One of them, John Prior, a carpenter from Manchester, lectured the Irish in what was later described as "an air of lofty benevolence." He thought it "disgraceful that for years past they of the Congress, speaking in the name of the toilers of the United Kingdom, had not been supported as they ought to have been by their Irish brethren." All he asked was "that the Irish give some help in the great work which the TUC had in hand."

Prior has been described by the Webbs, in their history of the British trade unions, as "one of the ablest disciples of the Junta." The Junta was a caucus of old-fashioned Liberal and Conservative working men who dominated the early TUC. Their young disciple Prior became general secretary of the Amalgamated Society of Carpenters and was later appointed one of Queen Victoria's Inspectors of Factories.

There is little more to be said about the British Trades Union Congress in Ireland. During its history the congress has met three times in this country—Dublin 1880, Belfast 1893, and Belfast again in 1929. But the delegates not only at the conferences in Ireland, but at all their conferences, spent little time discussing Irish affairs. Their conference arrangements committees generally put motions from Ireland and about Ireland at the bottom of the agenda so that they were not reached until Friday after lunch. By that time everyone was tired of passing resolutions and listening to speeches and wanted to get back home as quickly as possible.

This exasperated even the members of British unions in Ireland and in 1894 all the Irish unions decided to set up their own congress, the Irish TUC.

During the years 1856–60 the bakers' trade unions in Ireland organised a nation-wide campaign against night-work and Sunday-work that was important enough to be mentioned at length by Karl Marx in that part of his *Das Kapital* which deals with the working day. The bakers' campaign also caused parliament to appoint committees to inquire into the working conditions in bakehouses. It led to changes in the laws regulating bakeries.

The campaign opened when the Dublin bakers complained that they had to start work as early as three o'clock on Sunday afternoons and continue working through the night until late Monday morning and often until Monday afternoon. This made their working day anything between seventeen and twenty-two hours, during which time they were allowed only short breaks for meals and rest.

And where was the rest to be taken? In most bakehouses the only resting places were empty dough troughs. The bakers would be lucky to have a few folded flour sacks for pillows.

Some bakehouses, the bakers admitted, provided "the luxury of a bed" though the bed was generally placed in a loft above the ovens to which, as the bakers put it, "the unwholesome atmosphere ascends."

Bernard Hughes, master baker of Belfast and in his day one of the more humane and liberal-minded employers, thought that the long hours worked in the Dublin bakehouses resulted from the increased demand for bread in the previous ten years, and the failure of the master bakers of Dublin to meet this demand by providing more ovens and bakehouses, and employing more workmen. In a lecture, which he read to an audience in Dublin, he stated:

> The master bakers were anxious to make the most of the accommodation they had. The most probable way of doing this was to give the journeymen a few shillings extra each week to induce them to work the long hours and so take almost double the usual quantity of bread out of the same ovens.

Hughes thought that the practice of the Dublin master bakers was "an evil system, not to be tolerated in any Christian community." And he advised the journeymen bakers to put their case before the public through the medium of the newspapers and by means of public meetings. But what should be done if the masters did not change their methods? Then it was the duty of every humane person, said Hughes, to support the journeymen and lift his voice on their behalf.

Hughes seems to have convinced many people of the justice of the journeymen's case. In the Antient Concert Rooms, in May 1860, the Lord Mayor of Dublin presided at a public meeting called to support the journeymen in their demand for the abolition of night-work and Sunday-work in the bakeries. Among the speakers were Bernard Hughes himself, several Catholic and Protestant clergymen and Kells Ingram who is known to Irish Nationalists and Republicans as the author of the patriotic song 'Who Fears to Speak of Ninety-Eight,' and who was then a professor in Trinity College.

But despite the support of these influential people the journeymen bakers did not easily succeed in getting their hours of work reduced. The master bakers in Dublin defeated the campaign by dismissing and victimising the union leaders. The report of one of the committees set up by parliament to inquire into the bakeries in Ireland stated:

> In Dublin the master bakers have offered the most determined resistance to the movement, and by discountenancing as much as possible the journeymen promoting it have succeeded in leading the men into acquiescence in Sunday-work and night-work, contrary to the convictions of the men.

In Belfast the committee of the local union, the Operative Bakers, had already dealt effectively with the problem of Sunday-work. The secretary of the union said that they summoned "anyone found baking on Sunday or part thereof" and had them charged before the Police Court. There "by act of parliament every person so offending was liable to the penalty of not less than five shillings fine." He said that after one or two of these prosecutions had succeeded no journeyman baker in Belfast would dare to start work before midnight on Sunday.

The act of parliament which the Belfast bakers invoked in these cases had been passed in 1838. It was a comprehensive statute which not only forbade Sunday-work in bakehouses but also protected the public against adulterated bread, cakes and pies. It also re-enacted part of an Irish act of 1777 under which journeymen bakers could have been punished for "combining against their masters."

In those days a great many people, outside the ranks of the master bakers, believed that Sunday-work was a desecration of the Lord's Day. For example, the report of the committee on the Irish bakeries stated:

That for masters to induce their workmen, by fear of losing employment, to violate their religious convictions and their better feelings, to disobey the laws of the land and to disregard public opinion (all this refers to Sunday labour) is calculated to provoke ill-feeling between workmen and masters and affords an example dangerous to religion, morality and social order.

The report then denounced anything longer than a twelve-hour working day as "detrimental to family life and injurious to the health and welfare of the workmen." It asserted that excessively long hours of work caused premature senility and early death.

Marx noted that the journeymen bakers succeeded in their campaign against Sunday-work and night-work in the towns of Wexford, Kilkenny, Clonmel and Waterford. In these places, as well as in Belfast, "day labour alone was successfully established."

Elsewhere the journeymen failed and, as the committee of inquiry noted:

In Limerick where the grievances of the journeymen were demonstrated to be excessive, the movement has been defeated by the opposition of the master bakers, the miller bakers being the greatest opponents. The example in Limerick led to a retrogression in Ennis and Tipperary. In Cork, where the strongest possible demonstration of feeling took place, the masters by exerting their power of turning the men out of employment have defeated the movement.

In the mid-nineteenth century, by comparison with most other industries, the baking of bread was still a very backward business. The methods of preparing the dough and of making the bread had changed very little since the Middle Ages, or perhaps even since Roman times.

Then suddenly, in the middle of the journeymen's campaign for shorter hours, the bakehouses were offered dough-mixing machines that were capable of increasing output many times. In the Library of the Royal College of Surgeons in Dublin there is a booklet, written and published by John Jellico, a master baker of Harold's Cross, which describes two of these machines. One of them was operated by water-power and could produce 200 loaves, each two pounds in weight, within half-an-hour. The other machine was hand-operated and could produce between sixty and eighty loaves of the same weight in fifteen minutes.

Jellico was convinced, like Bernard Hughes, that better machinery was the best way to reduce working hours in the bakeries, better than acts of parliament.

But in the long run, despite the defeats they suffered in Dublin, Limerick, Cork and in the other places, the journeymen bakers succeeded in reducing the working day in their trade.

Several reports dealing with the bakeries were published between 1861 and 1863. They recommended, among other things, that no one under the age of eighteen years should be required to work at night, that the working day for juveniles and adults should not be more than ten hours, and that police officers should be given the power to enter bakehouses and enforce the existing law against Sunday work.

And in 1863 parliament passed the Bakehouses (Regulation) Act under which "any officer of health, inspector of nuisances, or other officer appointed by the local authority" could enter and inspect bakehouses.

7

THE FENIANS, PARNELL AND THE UNIONS

MANY of the Irishmen who went to Britain and to the USA during the nineteenth century had gained much political experience before they left their own country. A great number of the pre-Famine emigrants had been Ribbonmen, Whiteboys or had taken part in the Tithe War of the 1830s. Those who left Ireland after the Famine were either Fenians or became Fenians abroad. Wherever they went these Irishmen generally found employment as industrial workers, and so their energy for politics found a natural outlet in trade unionism and in socialist parties as well as in émigré societies whose main objective was to end British rule in Ireland.

The Molly Maguires, who fought a tough trade union campaign and who terrorised the mine-owners, blacklegs and labour-spies of Pennsylvania between 1850 and 1877, were originally Hibernians, Ribbonmen and Irish agitators of one sort and another. Murder, arson, sabotage and perjury were only some of the methods used by both sides in that long conflict. The Molly Maguires were eventually undermined and their leaders convicted and hanged through the work of hired infiltrators and spies like James McParlan from the Pinkerton Detective Agency.

While these rebel Irishmen abroad were foremost in the ranks of Labour and trade unionism their compatriots in the Orange Order were not so distinguished. In the early years of the nineteenth century, especially during the economic depression that followed the ending of the Napoleonic Wars in 1815, many Orangemen acted as spies and special constables assisting the English magistrates to suppress the Luddites.

The Luddites were misguided but desperate, redundant handicraftsmen who were convinced that machinery and factory production were the main causes of unemployment. They went about the country at dead of night wrecking machinery and setting factories on fire. Those Luddites who were caught were either hanged or transported for life.

In 1813 the Grand Orange Lodge of Ireland boasted that the Orangemen, including those who were special constables and government spies, "had saved their country by suppressing the treasonable bands calling themselves Luddites."

Six years later in Manchester, when the dragoons, acting on the orders of the local magistrates, sabred thousands of working-class demonstrators on St. Peter's Fields, the Orangemen, again in the role of special constables, charged in the rear of the government forces.

When the Irish Land League ostracised Captain Boycott of Lough Mask House, in 1880, the Orangemen of Ulster volunteered to save his harvest. Michael Davitt has described their arrival at Lough Mask, bedraggled and rain-soaked, under military escort.

The fifty volunteer Orange labourers from Ulster were escorted by a force of two thousand troops to Claremorris, in Mayo, and the tramp to Lough Mask, over a distance of fifteen miles, was to begin.

The troops and the Orangemen reached their destination soaked to the skin. Their welcome was not of the most hospitable kind, even at the hands of the man whom they had come to relieve and support.

The Fenian brotherhood, which began in West Cork in 1856, was a republican movement which earned the name of being socialistic. Three of the original Fenian leaders, James Stephens, Michael Doheny and John O'Mahony, had indeed been members of socialist societies in Paris during the early 'fifties. And John O'Leary in his *Recollections of Fenians and Fenianism* has described O'Mahony as "an advanced democrat of socialist opinion." Karl Marx wrote that "Fenianism was characterised by a socialistic tendency (in the negative sense directed against the appropriation of the soil) and by being a lower orders movement." The International Association of Working Men (the First International), in which Marx was a leading figure, supported the widespread campaign for the release of the Fenians who were imprisoned after the 1867 rising.

The Trinity College historian, William Edward Hartpole Lecky, referred in his writings to the "wild socialistic follies of Fenianism."

Dublin Castle, the higher Catholic and Protestant clergy, the landlords and the middle classes all regarded Fenianism as an offshoot of European Red Republicanism. They denounced Stephens as a communist, an anti-cleric and an agent of the Italian republican Giuseppe Garibaldi.

In 1865 when O'Donovan Rossa and his comrades were arrested and charged it was, in the words of Charles Barry, the Crown Prosecutor, for "inciting the lower orders to believe that they might expect a redistribution of property." Barry further accused the Fenians of "propagating socialism in its most pernicious and wicked phase" and of "teaching that the law by which any man possessed more property than another was unjust and wicked."

It was this propaganda which gave Fenianism the name of being socialistic. The founders of the brotherhood were middle-class intellectuals but the rank-and-file, it is true, were city workmen, small farmers and rural labourers. Michael Davitt, for example, was working in a Lancashire cotton factory when he joined the Fenian Brotherhood.

Yet although many working men were Fenians, including even some Protestant working men in the North, the Irish trade unions did not support the Fenian programme, no more than they had supported Chartism. In the 1860s the unions still upheld the economic nationalism which they had been advocating in the days of O'Connell.

In 1864, for instance, the unions in Dublin, especially the Corkcutters' Society, objected to the use of foreign corks in Irish bottles. And the Dublin United Trades Association supported the corkcutters in demanding that the Chancellor of the Exchequer protect the Irish corkcutting industry against foreign competition.

The United Trades Association also protested when "an ornamental and beautifully-wrought clock," donated by the Guinness family to St. Patrick's Cathedral, was imported from England. The association claimed that such a clock could have been made in Ireland.

On at least one occasion O'Connell, champion of economic nationalism that he was, had to defend himself against the accusation that he was spending too much money in London and not enough in Ireland. It was the Dublin Coachmakers' Union that accused him. They alleged that he had bought a carriage in London when he could easily have bought a similar carriage in Dublin. In reply O'Connell read out a list of the several carriages he had bought in Dublin and named the firms which had made them.

Economic nationalism on the part of the Irish trade unions was understandable. The more goods that could be produced locally, they argued with obvious common sense, the more employment would be given to local craftsmen.

But there were a few trade unionists whose political views were far in advance of this narrow-minded nationalism. In Belfast, for example, Frank Roney, an active member of the Friendly Society of Ironfounders, one of the amalgamated unions, was a Fenian organiser. In his autobiography, *Irish Rebel and Labor Leader*, Roney has recalled how the Belfast branch of his union was asked to send a delegate to an international conference in Geneva. The branch chose Roney because he seemed to be the most politically experienced member. But he was unable to attend. His Fenian activities took him elsewhere. This he afterwards regretted because the Geneva conference was the inaugural conference of the First International. He wrote:

It has been a matter of deep regret that I did not attend that conference. Garibaldi, with his crown of laurels freshly won as hero of united Italy, presided. Proudhon, the Frenchman and author of works on anarchism, and Bakunin, the Russian Nihilist, were there. I believe that Karl Marx, the father of scientific socialism, was also present as well as several advanced thinkers from among the trade unionists of England and other countries.

Roney was arrested for his Fenian activities in 1867 and, after spending several months in a Dublin prison, was allowed to emigrate to the USA. One of the conditions under which he was released was that he would never return to Ireland or to any part of the United Kingdom. He died at Long Beach, California, in 1925, at the age of eighty-four.

During the 1880s Roney became an outstanding trade union leader in San Francisco. Professor Ira B. Cross, the American historian who encouraged him to write his autobiography, has described him as "an idealist forced by the nature of events to fit into this earthly scheme of things." Cross also wrote:

In Ireland Roney sacrificed his earnings as a craftsman to help pay for the Fenian Rising. As a political leader in Nebraska his wages went to pay the costs of the campaign of the National Labor Reform Party. As a union leader in San Francisco he bore without complaint much of the expense of organising the trade unions in that city.

Jim Connell, born in Ireland in 1852, was another Fenian who became prominent in the Labour movement abroad. He is known throughout the world as the author of *The Red Flag*, the song that has been the anthem of British Labour for nearly ninety years.

In his young days Connell was a docker in Dublin where he joined a small group of socialists led by a man named John Lange. They used to discuss politics on long walks through the Dublin mountains on Sunday afternoons. Around 1900 Connell became secretary of a voluntary society which helped injured workmen to make claims for compensation against their employers—an early form of legal aid, in fact. In 1881 he was described by the commission which parliament set up to investigate 'Parnellism and Crime' as an "advocate of violence, assassination and terror" and was regarded as one of the revolutionaries with whom *The Times* had accused Parnell of associating.

Connell lived a long time. He was well known to that generation of Irish and British socialists and trade union leaders which included Jim Larkin, James Connolly, William O'Brien, Tom Mann, Pete Curran, Keir Hardie and others. Among his contemporaries was Robert Smillie who was born in Belfast, in 1857, who worked as a lad in the Belfast shipyards and who eventually became leader of the Scottish miners and a Labour member of the British House of Commons.

Connell died in London in 1929. Like Frank Roney in the USA he remained a socialist all his life. But neither his life nor the life of Frank Roney nor the early political activities of Stephens, Doheny and O'Mahoney nor the fulminations of Lecky, the Castle, the higher clergy and of Crown Prosecutor Barry make Fenianism a socialist movement. Fenianism undoubtedly had what Marx described as its 'socialistic tendency' but it goes down in history as the spearhead of Irish republicanism.

The one Fenian who was really close to the communist movement and who was in personal contact with Marx, Engels and the First International was John Patrick McDonnell, whom Marx nominated to be the International's corresponding secretary in Ireland. McDonnell sent reports to the International from early in 1871 until, towards the end of 1872, he emigrated to the United States of America. But little is known of him beyond the fact that he was a Fenian, a communist and an active member of the Labour movement in the USA.

In 1872 McDonnell invited a group of left-wing Irishmen then living in London, along with several continental socialists, to visit Ireland. In a message to the newspapers these men declared that they believed it their duty "to advocate the principle and the cause of the political and social revolution throughout the world." They formed branches of the International in Dublin and in Cork.

Michael Davitt in his book *The Fall of Feudalism in Ireland* has recorded a conversation during which Parnell described the trade unions as the landlords of labour. Davitt had requested an interview with Parnell to discuss the O'Shea divorce case and its possible repercussions in the Irish Parliamentary Party.

Before we talk on that subject [said Parnell], there is a matter I was to talk to you about. I don't approve of your labor organisation in the South of Ireland; it will lead to mischief and will do no good. What do the laborers and artisans want that we cannot obtain for them by the efforts of the National League as well if not better than through those of this new combination? I thought you were opposed to class movements? What is trade unionism but the landlordism of labor? I would not tolerate, if I were at the head of a government, such bodies as trade unions. They are opposed to individual liberty and should be kept down, as Bismarck keeps them down in Germany. He is quite right in his policy. Whatever has to be done for the protection of the working-class in the state should be the duty of the government and not the work of men like John Burns and others who will by-and-by, unless prevented, organise the working-classes into a power that will be too strong for the government to deal with. I would not allow that condition of things to grow up in Ireland, if I could prevent it in time, and I would most certainly try to do so. . . .

Davitt tried to say something in defence of the unions but Parnell ignored his objections.

There is another consideration I want to insist upon [Parnell said]. You are overlooking Mr. Gladstone's position and difficulties. Any agitation in Ireland, except one making directly for Home Rule, increases the obstacles he has to contend with over here. It diverts attention from the main issue of our movement, and your new labor organisation in Cork will frighten the capitalist Liberals and lead them to believe that a parliament in Dublin might be used for the purpose of furthering some kind of socialism. You ought to know that neither the Irish priests nor the farmers would support such principles. In any case your laborers and artisans who have waited so long for special legislation can put up with their present conditions until we get Home Rule. . . .

Whether Parnell was as anti-union as this tirade against Davitt would suggest is another question. It is a fact that, in 1891, he spoke at a conference in Dublin of the General Labourers' and Gasworkers' Union and declared his support for the universal franchise, for free trade unions, for working-class MPs, for legislation to enforce the eight-hour day in industry, and even for the nationalisation of railways, canals and the land.

At that time, with the Irish Parliamentary Party divided over the O'Shea divorce scandal and his own political career in ruins, Parnell was seeking friends and allies everywhere and even thought of joining forces with the Fenian revolutionaries at home and abroad. That is one possible explanation for his radical speech to the general labourers and gasworkers. Parnell was anything but a socialist.

Davitt, on the other hand, had been an active social-democrat since about 1882. During the last twenty years of his life, until his death in 1906, he attended many trade union conferences in Britain, encouraged trade unionism in Ireland and often spoke in support of Labour candidates for parliament. Like Fergus O'Connor, he was convinced that the Irish would find their most reliable allies in the British working class. Between 1882 and 1884 he travelled to many towns in England and Scotland, where there were large numbers of Irish workers, to speak about trade unionism, Labour politics and Home Rule for Ireland.

Apparently these activities displeased Parnell who rejected all talk of an alliance of Irish Nationalists and British Labour, and scornfully remarked in 1884 that:

We are told of some great wave of English democracy that is coming over to assist the Irish democracy. The poor Irish democracy will have, I fear, to rely upon themselves in the future as they have had to do up to the present.

Perhaps Parnell had good reason for being scornful of British trade union leaders. In the 1870s and 1880s these union leaders had little knowledge of Ireland and no interest either in its people or in its economic problems. Indeed union leaders like Henry Broadhurst, a stonemason who became an under-secretary in one of Gladstone's governments and who used to spend weekends with the Prince of Wales at Windsor Castle, detested the Irish Land League and consistently opposed Home Rule.

But despite the views of men like Broadhurst, Davitt continued to uphold the principles of Labour and believed they could be applied in Ireland. In his paper, *Labour World,* which ran from September 1890 until May 1891, he called for:

The better and more democratic organisation of labour,
The more equitable distribution of the products of industry and agriculture,
More public ownership of such monopolies as can be managed by public bodies in the public interest.

Davitt, whose forebears had been small farmers in Co. Mayo, was concerned about the plight of the rural labourers of whom there were, in his time, about 300,000 in the whole of Ireland. These labourers were scattered, extremely poor and servile, and driven by circumstances either to emigrate or to seek seasonal employment with farmers in Britain.

In 1873 an Irish Agricultural Labourers' Union was started in Munster with the help of W. C. Upton, a carpenter who lived in Limerick; Isaac Butt, the Home Rule politician; and Joseph Arch, leader of the agricultural workers in England. Three thousand people attended the inaugural conference of this union at Kanturk, Co. Cork, but despite what seemed to be an encouraging start the union failed and within a few months had disappeared.

Davitt went to Cork in January 1890, to set up what he called the Irish Democratic Trade and Labour Federation. This was really a trade union for agricultural workers; it was, in fact, the "labor organisation in the South of Ireland" which Parnell thought would lead to mischief and do no good. As it happened, Davitt's attempts to organise the agricultural labourers also failed.

A few months later he suggested to some trade union leaders in Dublin that they should consider forming an all-Ireland trade union federation. The Dublin leaders called a meeting to discuss this suggestion and so prepared the way for the Irish Trades Union Congress, which was set up in 1894.

From the beginning of the 1890s Davitt spent much time in trade union activity. He was chosen to arbitrate in a docks strike in Liverpool. He represented the builders' labourers of Dublin when they were in a dispute with the master builders. He addressed several meetings of the Irish railway workers when they were on strike against the Great Southern and Western Railway. In 1890 he was invited to address the May Day Labour rally in Hyde Park, London.

But with all his interest in the unions he refused to attend an eve-of-conference rally organised by the General Labourers' and Gas Workers' Union in 1891. In fact he told the organisers of the rally that while he was willing at all times to work alongside British trade unions he did not think they had any right to organise in Ireland. Another reason for his declining the invitation may have been that Parnell was also invited.

Davitt insisted that trade unions in Ireland should be independent of British control, that they should manage their own funds, and should not be compelled to take action merely because a committee in London, unacquainted with industrial conditions in Ireland, said that was what they should do. His views on these matters have influenced members of Irish—as distinct from British—trade unions in Ireland to the present day.

Davitt did not always agree with Keir Hardie and other early Labour Party leaders, because he was inclined to the view, especially during the early 1890s, that an Independent Labour Party was premature. Yet he lived to see the day when, due in no small measure to his work, the Irish voters in Britain helped to return twenty-nine Independent Labour members and eleven Liberal-Labour members to the Westminster parliament. That was in the general election of 1906. Davitt was one of the honoured guests who attended the Labour Party's victory celebrations in London. A few months later he died from an infection of the lower-jaw which developed after he had had a tooth extracted by a so-called painless dentist in Dublin.

8

THE LAW AND THE IRISH TUC

NOTHING of much importance happened in the Irish trade union movement from the time of the Fenians until the formation of the Irish Trades Union Congress in 1894. In 1871 the British parliament, acting on the recommendations of a Royal Commission that had inquired into trade unionism, passed the Trade Union Act. This act, sometimes called the Charter of Trade Unionism, gives the unions legal status and defines a trade union as "any combination either temporary or permanent" which is set up to:

Regulate relations between workmen and employers, workmen and workmen, or employers and employers,
Impose restrictions on the conduct of any trade or business,
Provide benefits to members.

Before the Trade Union Act was passed the unions were scarcely lawful. Union activities, insofar as they aimed to force employers to pay higher wages, reduce hours of work and restrict apprentices, had been interpreted by generations of magistrates as conspiracies. The unions were held to be guilty of such common law offences as intimidation, inducing breach of contract, or acting in restraint of trade.

The Trade Union Act sets aside these interpretations by stating that "the purposes of a trade union shall not, by reason merely that they are in restraint of trade, be deemed to be unlawful."

The act also encourages trade unions to register with the Registrar-General of Friendly Societies. Registration is not compulsory but it brings certain advantages and so most trade unions are registered unions.

The Trade Union Act applied to Ireland from the day it became law and is now, as in Britain, the basic law that defines and protects trade unions in Northern Ireland and in the Republic of Ireland. If, however, the Republic of Ireland and Northern Ireland introduce laws similar to the 1971 Industrial Relations Act in Britain the act of 1871 and some other statutes regulating trade unions will be repealed and a new system of labour law set up.

While it had jurisdiction over all Ireland the Westminster

parliament passed other trade union laws. Of these the most important are the Trades Disputes Act (1906) and the Trade Union Act (1913), both of which are operative in Ireland, North and South.

The 1906 act absolves the trade unions from being sued by employers or others who may suffer material loss as a result of trade disputes; it also defines trade disputes and authorises peaceful picketing.

The act of 1913 extends the definition of trade union contained in the act of 1871 to cover any lawful activity. Thus this act gives the unions the right to raise political funds and to engage in political activities.

Since 1920 the Twenty-six Counties of Ireland have been free to make their own trade union laws or to amend the laws inherited from the British. As it happened the continuance of the British laws was accepted by the Government of the Irish Free State in 1922. They were reaffirmed in the Constitution of Eire in 1937.

The 1937 constitution also guarantees the right of every citizen to form associations and unions provided, of course, their purpose is lawful. This right was upheld, in 1943, when the National Union of Railwaymen, a British union which then had members in Ireland, claimed that the Constitution was being violated by Part Three of Acht Ceard-Chumann (the Trade Union Act) of 1941.

Part Three provided for "the establishment of a tribunal having power to restrict the right of organisation of trade unions." It was repealed following the success of the NUR's case.

Acht Ceard-Chumann and the Industrial Relations Act of 1946 are the only major labour laws passed in Southern Ireland since the end of British rule.

The 1941 act, as it remains after the repeal of Part Three, defines the difference between British unions in Ireland and Irish unions. It provides for "the licensing of bodies which carry on negotiations for the fixing of wages and conditions of employment." The 1946 act created a Labour Court for the investigation and settling of trade disputes.

Under the terms of the Government of Ireland Act (1920) the Parliament of Northern Ireland also has the right to legislate on labour matters, but, for obvious political reasons, Stormont cannot afford to allow its labour legislation to diverge far from the laws of Britain. There are, however, a few disparities. These reflect the basically anti-Labour outlook of the Ulster Unionists.

One example is the Trade Disputes and Trade Union Act of 1927. In 1926 the British trade unions were involved in the General Strike and as a consequence the Westminster parliament passed the Trade Disputes Act. This law curbed the right of civil servants to belong to unions which were affiliated to the TUC. It put restrictions on the political freedoms which the unions had been granted in 1913.

Northern Ireland was not directly implicated in the General Strike, yet the Stormont parliament following "step-by-step with Britain" passed its own Trade Disputes Act, worded exactly like the British act.

In 1945 the British parliament repealed the 1927 act but Stormont refused to repeal any part of its act until 1958 and only then because it had become inoperative. To the present day, however, the law in Northern Ireland restricts the unions' freedom to raise political funds.

The Trade Union Act of 1871 probably had the effect of bringing some old Irish unions into alliance and amalgamation with kindred unions in Britain. During the last twenty-five years of the nineteenth century many Irish craft unions merged with British unions. In 1890 two of the newly-formed general unions in Britain, the National Union of Dock Labourers and the Gasworkers' and General Labourers' Union, began to recruit members in Ireland, with considerable success.

In 1898 the Registrar-General of Friendly Societies stated, in his annual report, that "the great majority of organised workers in Ireland were associated with British societies."

Nonetheless there were still many independent Irish unions. Some, like the union for Dublin paviors, were small in membership; others were fairly large. The Dublin United Builders' Labourers' Society had 2,500 members in the 1880s; the Dublin Quay Labourers' Society had 1,500 members.

Furthermore, local unions of skilled craftsmen continued to be formed in many parts of Ireland during those years. There were unions for brewery workers in Dublin and in Cork, unions for municipal employees in Belfast, Dublin, Cork and Limerick, and unions for dockers, building-trade workers and linen operatives.

In 1889 the Belfast United Trades Council, which had been set up in 1881, assisted the lightermen on the River Lagan to form a union. A few years later the council started a union for Belfast's dock labourers. In 1893 it helped women workers in the linen industry to set up the Textile Operatives' Society. At that time there were ten small unions in the linen industry, with a total membership of about 5,000.

During the last decade of the nineteenth century there was a very rapid growth in trade union membership and, by 1900, fifty-seven unions, representing a total membership of 19,000, were affiliated to the Belfast United Trades Council. Twenty-five of these were local unions.

By that time the trades council was reorganised in Dublin, while new trades councils had sprung up in Drogheda, Kilkenny, Cork, Limerick, Newry and Waterford.

Meanwhile the struggles within industry continued. In 1895–96 the Belfast members of the Amalgamated Society of Engineers were involved in a dispute during which a secret anti-union agreement between the shipbuilding employers of Belfast and the Clyde was exposed. The ASE was then one of the most militant unions in Ireland, with seventy-five per cent of its 3,000 Irish membership in Belfast. "Their organisatión," wrote J. B. Jeffries in *The Story of the Engineers,* "could be described as next door to perfect."

In September 1895 the ASE on the Clyde asked for a minimum wage of 7½d. an hour, or £1.13.9. for the fifty-four hour week then being worked in shipbuilding and engineering. The Clyde men eventually accepted a smaller increase.

A month later the Belfast members of the ASE asked for the restoration of a two shillings reduction which they had been forced to accept in 1893, but when Belfast ASE pressed this demand the employers referred to an agreement which they claimed bound them to pay wages no higher than what the Clyde Employers' Association was willing to pay.

The Executive Council of the ASE, much against the wishes of the Belfast members, eventually agreed to meet the Belfast employers and the Clyde employers at a conference in Carlisle. There the Executive Council accepted an offer which did not satisfy the Belfast members. Consequently members of the union in the Belfast shipbuilding industry came out on strike.

It was then that the union and the general public got a shock; they saw industrial blackmail in action. As soon as the Belfast men downed tools the Clyde employers posted notices to the effect that for every week the Belfast ASE remained on strike twenty-five per cent of the union's membership on the Clyde would be dismissed.

And so began a struggle in which the employers' side was described as "the strongest combination ever banded together to crush trade unionism." Three thousand ASE members in both ports were involved, along with at least 1,300 non-union men.

The employers found that even the newspapers, upon whose support they could usually rely during trade disputes, were none too sympathetic in this case. *The Financial News* described the Clyde-Belfast employers' agreement as cowardly and a disgrace even to the sordid history of trade disputes.

This unfavourable publicity compelled the employers to seek another conference with the union. The Lord Mayor of Belfast, the Lord Mayor of Glasgow and Lord James of Hereford had each intervened in an effort to reach a settlement, but the Belfast men refused all offers from the employers. They insisted on the minimum of 7½d. an hour.

The Executive Council of the ASE accepted the employers' second and more favourable offer, despite the opposition of the Belfast members, and ended the strike by cutting off the strike pay, thus forcing the majority of members in Belfast and on Clydeside to return to work.

In 1901 the North of Ireland Operative Butchers' Society, a local union, was involved in a lawsuit that has become world-famous and has been studied by generations of lawyers in many countries. The case arose out of an attempt by J. Quinn and other officials of the union to compel Leatham, a flesher operating in the Belfast Abattoir, to employ only union labour. The case is listed in the law records as Quinn v. Leatham.

Leatham refused to dismiss some of his workmen who had been expelled from the union for not paying their contributions. He tried, however, to encourage them to rejoin the union and even offered to pay their arrears of contributions. But the union rejected this offer and in the course of the dispute that followed Quinn and his colleagues persuaded Munroe, a meat-retailer, not to take supplies from Leatham.

When Munroe stopped buying meat Leatham brought an action against the union officials on the grounds that they had conspired together to injure him and that, as a result, he had suffered material damage. The case was tried by a judge and jury who found for Leatham and awarded him £250 damages. The union appealed against this decision and took the appeal to the House of Lords. The Lords upheld the jury's verdict.

The Quinn v. Leatham case established—and this is presumably where it is of interest to lawyers—that "if two or more persons combine together, without legal justification, to injure another and by doing so cause him damage, they are liable in an action for conspiracy."

A few months after the case of Quinn v. Leatham the House of Lords awarded the Taff Vale Railway Company, in South Wales, a total of £40,000 in damages and costs against the Amalgamated Society of Railway Servants. The union in this case had called a strike, and had tried to prevent non-union labour being employed by the company. The company claimed they had suffered loss of revenue as a result of the union's action.

The Taff Vale judgement, as well as the decision in the case of Quinn v. Leatham, very much alarmed the trade unions. They could see these judgements undermining the protection they believed had been given to them by the 1871 Trade Union Act. If the Taff Vale judgement stood, strikes would be impossible. Employers could sue the unions every time there was a withdrawal of labour.

The Taff Vale case led almost directly to the passing of the 1906 Trades Disputes Act, but even that law has, in recent years, been the cause of much legal controversy. It was challenged by the House of Lords in their Rookes-Barnard judgement in 1962, reaffirmed by an Act of the British parliament in 1965, examined by the Royal Commission that inquired into British trade unions between 1966 and 1969, and has now been repealed by the British Industrial Relations Act of 1971. In the Republic of Ireland the original 1906 Act remains intact and will, presumably, continue so until Dail Eireann decides otherwise.

The men who formed the Irish Trades Union Congress in 1894 were nearly all members of British craft unions. Some of them, like Samuel Monroe, a Belfast printer, were working-class Conservatives. Many of the others, if they had any firm political views at all, were adherents of the Irish Parliamentary Party. Only a few of the ITUC's original members belonged to local Irish unions.

The Irish TUC was not set up in any spirit of Irish Nationalism nor did the men who formed the congress intend that it should supersede the British TUC. Their reasons for creating the congress were practical, not in the least ideological.

For one thing, most of the trade unions in Ireland found they could ill afford the expense of sending delegates to the annual conferences of the British TUC. And even those unions who could afford to send delegates thought that they in Ireland got little, if any, benefit from the British congress. This was because of the British TUC's habit of putting motions about Ireland to the bottom of the agenda or of referring them "back to the Parliamentary Committee for further consideration." The Irish business was shelved or forgotten about until it was perhaps raised the following year. "The tangle of Irish agrarian and political problems bored and irritated the British."

The only real interest that the British TUC had in anything Irish was to make sure that Irish workers in Britain were organised into trade unions so that they would not undercut the wages of British workers.

In 1895, at the second conference of the Irish TUC in Cork, it was stated that the British Congress could not be of any help to the trade unions in Ireland. In the opinion of many of the delegates at Cork the British TUC had become "top heavy and overladen with bureaucracy and was engrossed in a multitude of duties and interests." Furthermore, they repeated, delegates from Ireland could not possibly hope to make even the slightest impression on the British TUC.

The Cork conference decided, therefore, that it would be in the best interests of the Irish unions to maintain the Irish TUC. Subsequent annual conferences rejected all suggestions that the Irish TUC be disbanded and the unions renew their direct links with the British TUC.

Apart from this firm refusal to be reassimilated with the British, the Irish TUC avoided all controversial political questions. For many years its annual agenda dealt mainly with wages, working conditions, technical education, the inspection, safety and legal control of factories and workshops—in fact all the usual matters that trade unions nearly everywhere are interested in.

9

LABOUR POLITICS

FOR almost the first twenty years of its history the Irish TUC maintained a sort of political truce with, on the one side, those who stood for Home Rule and, on the other, the Unionists, or Conservatives, who were convinced that Ireland was better off as "an integral part of the United Kingdom."

It was not until Larkin and Connolly rose to prominence in the Irish Labour movement that the annual conferences of the Irish TUC became markedly political in tone. The formation of the Irish Transport and General Workers' Union, in 1909, was to change the political direction of the trade union movement in Ireland.

Three years after its formation the Irish Transport Union promoted a resolution, at the Clonmel conference of the Irish

TUC, which called for the setting up of the Irish Labour Party.

By 1914—the year when the First World War broke out—there were three distinct political groupings within the Irish trade union movement. These were firstly the Home Rulers, secondly the pro-British Unionists, and thirdly the socialists, though the socialists themselves were somewhat divided on the question of Home Rule or union with Britain.

Socialist thought in Ireland may be traced back to the 1840s, as Desmond Greaves has stated in his *Life and Times of James Connolly,* but at no time, and least of all today, have the socialists of Ireland enjoyed much support from the working people.

Indeed one of the political wonders of the twentieth century is the persistence with which the industrial workers of Belfast, a city where trade unions are well organised and not unaware of their industrial rights and interests, send Tory politicians to the Northern Ireland and Westminster parliaments. It is, of course, only the Protestant working men who vote Tory. The Catholics have been Labour supporters for more than fifty years.

Writing of the Irish Labour movement as it was in the latter half of the nineteenth century Clarkson noted that "radical views were confined to a small assorted group of socialists, atheists, anarchists and stray Fenians." And among these radicals were men like Jim Connell, Frank Roney and John Patrick McDonnell. Earlier Irish radicals, those whom Greaves refers to as having been active in the 1840s, were generally Chartists. The communist groups formed by McDonnell in the early 1870s were denounced, as the Chartists were, by the clergy, the newspapers and the politicians. The Royal Irish Constabulary offered no protection when the comrades of the First International were attacked by mobs in the streets of Dublin and Cork.

With McDonnell's emigration to the USA the influence of the First International declined in Ireland. During the 'seventies and 'eighties whatever socialist thought prevailed in the country derived from the English Fabian Society or from the London-based Social Democratic Federation. A small group of Social Democrats, Jim Connell among them, met frequently in Dublin during the 'seventies.

There was a sprinkling of socialists and social democrats in the Irish trade union movement during the 1880s. In 1885, on the eve of the first Home Rule crisis, Alexander Bowman, secretary of the Belfast United Trades Council, became the first Irish working man to stand for parliament. He was nominated for North Belfast, not as a socialist, however, but as the official

Liberal Party candidate. His Unionist opponent, Sir William Ewart, won the election by a three-to-one majority.

Ewart was one of the biggest linen employers in the North. Bowman was merely a linen worker. He had been a flax dresser in one of Ewart's mills. His home in North Belfast was often attacked by mobs of Orange loyalists.

Alexander Bowman gave many years' service to the trade union movement. He was one of six trade unionists who successfully fought the Belfast municipal elections in 1898, and who were the first Labour men in history to become members of Belfast Corporation.

In those days various sorts of Left-wing groups were meeting in Belfast and in Dublin. J. W. Boyle has pointed out, in an article entitled *The Irish Labour Movement 1880–1907*, that in Dublin a branch of the Social Democratic Federation was founded on the membership of an already existing Dublin Socialist Union. The Socialist Union claimed continuity with "earlier radical and socialist parties."

In 1894 the Dublin Social Democratic Federation became the Dublin branch of the Independent Labour Party. Two years earlier the Belfast Fabian Society had become the Belfast branch of the ILP.

The Fabian societies, the social democratic groups and the branches of the Independent Labour Party were all, more or less, offshoots of socialist movements in Britain. There was another group in Dublin, the Socialist Club, and it was this group which in 1896 invited James Connolly from Edinburgh to become its organiser, at a salary of £1 a week, to be paid when the money could be raised.

This marked the beginning of Connolly's political life in Ireland. He had already been active in the socialist movement in Scotland, had stood as a Labour candidate in the Edinburgh municipal elections and had been denied employment as a result. Within a few weeks of his arrival in Dublin, and after getting himself and his family of young children settled in a working-class house, he launched the Irish Socialist Republican Party and issued a manifesto.

Like *The People's Charter*, the Manifesto of the Irish Socialist Republican Party was ahead of the times. It was revolutionary when it first appeared; today it would be considered quite moderate. Indeed its proposals are now part of everyday life. The manifesto proposed, among other things, nationalisation of transport, graduated income tax, old-age pensions, family allowances, elected local boards to supervise education, votes for all adults, and free education up to university standard. Society has accepted all these reforms as it has long accepted the points of *The People's Charter*.

Yet in 1896 the Manifesto of the Irish Socialist Republican Party was read by only a very small number of working people in Dublin. The recently-formed Irish TUC, dominated as it was by responsible trade union leaders, was certainly not then ready to consider anything so advanced as nationalisation of transport, free university education or family allowances.

Three years earlier, in 1893, when the British TUC held its annual conference in Belfast, the top leaders of the Independent Labour Party had been in Ireland. Never before in the history of Belfast had there been so many socialist politicians all together in the city. Keir Hardie was there; John Burns, the MP for Battersea; Will Thorne, Ben Tillett, leader of the London dockers; James Sexton, secretary of the dockers' union in Liverpool and the man who was in later years to dismiss Jim Larkin from his post as union organiser in Ireland, were only some of the well-known British Labour leaders who came to Belfast with the TUC.

At the end of the week when the congress had finished its business the Belfast branch of the Independent Labour Party organised a march through East Belfast, a part of the city inhabited mainly by shipyard workers. The venue was a rally in the Ormeau Park.

The shipyard men, many of whom were members of the Orange Order, were quite furious when they learned that a Labour procession was to pass by their houses, and that notorious supporters of Irish Home Rule, namely Hardie, Burns and Will Thorne, would be leading the procession. And so the Orangemen lay in wait for the marchers and attacked them as they passed along Templemore Avenue. They attacked again when the procession reached Ormeau Park, broke up the Labour rally and threatened to throw John Burns into the River Lagan.

The Independent Labour Party at that time had indeed the reputation of being in favour of Home Rule for Ireland though at least one party member at whom such an accusation could hardly have been levelled was William Walker, a carpenter who rose to prominence in the Belfast Labour movement in the early years of this century.

Walker, a clever and persistent organiser and an effective public speaker, was in time to become a member of Belfast Corporation and to serve on the Board of Poor Law Guardians. The political viewpoint which he held most firmly was that

Labour in Ireland should not be a separatist movement acting independently of British Labour and chasing the myth of a free state in Ireland. He believed that Home Rule would be disastrous for Ireland, and purported not to understand those socialists like James Connolly who thought that Irish political independence should be high on the programme of the Irish Labour movement.

Walker became a member of the Executive Committee of the British Labour Party and stood as official Labour candidate, three times in North Belfast and once for Leith Burghs in Edinburgh. At the annual conferences of the Irish TUC he persistently opposed all motions for the setting up of a Labour Party in Ireland.

In 1906 Walker came within a few hundred votes of winning North Belfast, but in a by-election the following year he ruined a good campaign by succumbing to the pressure of the Belfast Protestant Association, a militantly anti-Catholic organisation. The association presented Walker with a list of questions about nuns and convents and the political influence of the Catholic clergy. The answers which he gave were very offensive to Catholics. They revealed his basic religious bigotry and lost him thousands of votes. Had he been a wiser politician he may well have won North Belfast and become Ireland's first Labour MP. His Unionist opponent, Sir Daniel Dixon, simply ignored the Protestants' questionnaire, and won the election.

Walker became a full-time official of the woodworkers' union but he left that job, in 1912, to take up a post as an official in the government's national insurance scheme. He died in 1918, still a comparatively young man, in his late forties.

William Walker's political philosophy, if an outlook based upon the prejudices of the Protestant working class can be called a philosophy, found other adherents in later years. Henry Cassidy Midgley, for example, held the pro-British view so strongly that, in 1944, he left the Northern Ireland Labour Party to form what he called the Commonwealth Labour Party. Later he abandoned the Labour movement altogether to become a member of the Stormont Unionist Cabinet and a faithful follower of the Orange Order.

The Walker-Midgley philosophy has dominated the Northern Ireland Labour Party since 1949. It has turned that unfortunate organisation into something little better than a shadow of Ulster Unionism. It has kept Labour in the North divided into partitionist and anti-partition factions and prevented the creation of a united Catholic-Protestant working-class opposition to the Unionist Party. It is one of the least inspiring aspects of politics in Northern Ireland.

10

LARKIN IN BELFAST

THE years 1907 and 1913 are outstanding in Irish trade union history for they are the years in which the unskilled labourers, at first in Belfast and then in Dublin, asserted their right to belong to trade unions. In each city this right was bitterly resisted by the employers—the Orange employers in Belfast, the Catholic employers in Dublin. On the workers' side was Jim Larkin, who came from Liverpool. He led the struggles for free trade unionism and will be remembered as long as there is a Labour movement in Ireland.

Larkin arrived in Belfast early in 1907 as organiser for the National Union of Dock Labourers; his mission was to create a trade union for the dock-labourers, carters and coal-fillers of the city. He had been appointed organiser in Liverpool, against the wishes, it seems, of James Sexton, general secretary of the Dock Labourers, though Sexton later admitted that Larkin was remarkably successful at organising non-union labour. Consequently the appointment, which was temporary at first, was made permanent. That was in the year 1905.

The following year, 1906, saw a general election for the British House of Commons, and Larkin acted as Sexton's agent in the Toxteth (Liverpool) constituency. Sexton later wrote in his autobiography, that:

Larkin displayed an energy that was almost superhuman. . . . The division was one of the storm centres of religious strife and a stronghold of the Orange Order. My being a Roman Catholic made the situation still more lively. But nothing could frighten Jim. He plunged recklessly into the fray where the fighting was most furious, organised gigantic processions, faced mobs saturated with religious bigotry who were howling for our blood and competed with our opponents in the risky game of impersonation then played at almost every election in Liverpool.

Larkin's early days were obscure. He was the son of an Irish emigrant in Liverpool and in his youth had been an errand-boy, a stowaway and a seaman. When Sexton first met him he was a kind of foreman over dock-labourers on the Liverpool water-front, what was called locally a 'cod-boss.' Around that time he led a strike to compel some of the other cod-bosses to join the union. The strike was unsuccessful but through it he became a union organiser.

Though Sexton admired Larkin's energy, courage and enthusiasm he could hardly be described as one of his friends. In fact he rather regarded him as "a strange mixture of the swaggering swashbuckler and the none-too-scrupulous fighter for whatever side he chose—and that side (Sexton added) was usually Jim Larkin's side." This suggests that in Sexton's opinion Larkin was interested only in himself; yet, as R. M. Fox has pointed out in his biography of Larkin, it was Sexton who was eventually awarded a knighthood for his Labour activities and not Jim Larkin.

Larkin was a natural leader of men. He had the advantage of great height (being over six feet tall), a powerful voice and outstanding courage. Even what Sexton thought was his unscrupulousness might have made him a better fighter. His years in the leadership of Irish Labour, few though they were, won him the admiration of men like Sean O'Casey and Frank O'Connor. He inspired them and others to write plays and poems and books; yet some of his closest colleagues in the Irish trade unions, apart altogether from Sexton, thought him nothing but a dictator and an opportunist. Perhaps Larkin, like many men of action, was impatient with, and intolerant of people who were less militant than himself.

For generations before Larkin came into their city the working people of Belfast had been murdering and maiming one another in the name of religion. The Protestants believed all Catholics to be disloyal. They lived in fear of what they thought were 'popish superstitions.' And because of this fear they were quickly incited to violence by fanatical clergymen and Unionist politicians. Year after year they turned the overcrowded slums which were their homes, and the factories and shipyards where they spent most of their dreary lives into scenes of fearful rioting and destruction. In such circumstances it was almost impossible to create an independent working-class movement.

One of Larkin's achievements was that in the brief summer of 1907 he united the people of Belfast into an effective Labour movement. He had the Catholics and the Protestants, the Orangemen, Hibernians, republicans and socialists all marching together and demonstrating through the city in defence of trade union rights. And this movement which he created was met by the combined opposition of the employers, the civil authorities, the police and the armed forces.

Larkin had been in Belfast only a few weeks and was making progress in his work of organising the dockers into the union when the Unionist newspapers began denouncing him as 'a socialist and a Catholic' and warning Protestant working men not to join in his agitations. The workers replied to this by re-affirming Larkin as their leader and by taking part in a non-sectarian Labour demonstration on the very eve of the Orange celebrations of 12 July.

The employers and the authorities had been relying on the Orange parades to rouse sectarian bitterness and so undermine the trade union. They were downcast when the Independent Orangemen, who had broken away from the orthodox Orange Order in 1903, collected money for the Larkin strike fund along the route of their march. St. John Ervine, the Belfast playwright who was in those days a socialist but who later turned Unionist, wrote a play entitled *Mixed Marriage* which exposed the Orange employers' attempts to wreck Larkin.

Since 6 May the docks of Belfast had been brought almost to a standstill by a strike which started with the dock-labourers and spread to the coal-fillers and carters. It spread also to the girls working in Gallaher's tobacco factory because Tom Gallaher, owner of the factory, was a director of the Belfast Steamship Company with which the dockers were in dispute. Larkin urged the tobacco-workers to form a trade union and to strike in sympathy with the dockers. A few days later he organised Gallaher's workers in Derry.

The docks strike started, perhaps prematurely, when the union men refused to work alongside non-union labour; but next morning when, on Larkin's instructions, they reported back to work the union men found themselves locked out and their jobs taken by strike-breakers who had been imported overnight from Liverpool.

From that moment the excitement in Belfast increased. Thousands of extra policemen and soldiers were drafted into the city to protect the strike-breakers and to convey blackleg lorries and vans to and from the docks. Every day, vast crowds of dockers on strike, along with their supporters, gathered near the sheds of the Belfast Steamship Company or at the Custom House steps to hear Larkin's reports.

The Royal Sussex Regiment, from which the first drafts of troops were drawn, set up field headquarters on the dockside and installed signalling equipment to keep in touch with the military barracks at Holywood, on the other side of Belfast Lough.

Larkin put forward three demands: freedom of the workers to join the union; a wage increase that would bring the rate for dockers up to sixpence an hour, plus another threepence for overtime; and the removal of the Liverpool strike-breakers. Early in the dispute he succeeded in getting one of the coal-importing firms to agree to these terms, but the other shipping companies resisted and, on 11 July, issued a document which every worker who wanted his job back was expected to sign.

The document stated that "no person representing any union or combination would be recognised by the employers," that the employers would exercise the right to employ or dismiss whom they chose, and that if a strike took place without three days' written notice the men on strike would be locked out and their jobs given to others. The workers were given until 15 July to consider and accept these conditions. They rejected them; Larkin burned a copy of the document at a meeting near the docks.

Meanwhile the employers were recruiting more strike-breakers, many of whom were attacked in the streets leading to the docks and the vans they drove overturned and set on fire. Several strike-breakers were driven from the public-houses along the dockside when they ventured beyond the protection of the police and military cordons. Larkin himself had to stand trial for an alleged attack on one of them.

Almost daily from the commencement of the strike he held mass meetings and reported on what was happening. At these meetings he attacked the authorities, the police and the employers in language that was far from moderate. He described Tom Gallaher, for example, as 'an obscene scoundrel' and said that "although St. Patrick was credited with having banished reptiles from Ireland there was one he forgot and that was Gallaher—a man who valued neither country, God, nor creed."

He produced a letter, dated 1 May, which the Shipping Federation in London had sent to the Belfast employers, pledging full support in the fight against the union and offering to recruit non-union labour should there be a dispute. Larkin exposed the fact that this letter was written five days before the strike started. He also warned the authorities that should they send out hussars or dragoons to ride down the workers he would know what to do. He assured them that the horses, innocent animals though they were, would be crippled with paving-stones and squaresets dug up from the roadways.

Early in the course of the strike the soldiers had tried to stop pickets of union men from entering the dock area, but Larkin approached the officers in command and read to them those parts of the 1906 Trades Disputes Act which allowed peaceful picketing. After that the pickets were allowed past the military cordons.

Many organisations sent money to help the strikers. Belfast Trades Council collected £100 and set itself the target of another £4,000. Belfast branches of the Amalgamated Society of Carpenters and Joiners levied their members the astonishingly high sum of three shillings a week for the strike fund. Linen workers in Jennymount Mills, though poorly paid themselves, each gave a weekly subscription. The Belfast railwaymen asked the executive council of their union, the Amalgamated Society of Railway Servants, to donate £1,000.

During the strike the Dungannon Club, whose members in Belfast included Sean MacDiarmada, Bulmer Hobson, Robert Lynd and other well-known republicans, published a leaflet in support of Larkin and invited him to give a lecture on the aims of the Labour movement.

Towards the end of July the strike, which by then involved 2,500 dockers, carters and coal-fillers, looked like being settled by arbitration—when suddenly the dispute spread to the Royal Irish Constabulary in Belfast. The constables had long-standing grievances about pay, hours of duty and general conditions. They could get no satisfaction even though a commission of inquiry had reported on these matters at the beginning of that year. Conditions were worse, of course, during the dockers' strike when the police were compelled to undertake the extra duty of protecting the non-union men.

On 16 July Larkin remarked, in one of his speeches, that the police were working eighteen hours a day and were not receiving an extra penny in pay. A few days later, led by their spokesman, Constable Barrett, the men of the RIC presented their demands in the form of an ultimatum to the police chiefs in Belfast. This action was regarded by the authorities as mutiny. But when they tried to suspend Barrett and several others, the entire police force held a strike meeting in the yard of Musgrave Street barracks. During this meeting they manhandled and, it was alleged, 'knocked down' the Acting Commissioner, Henry B. Morell.

After this the suspension notices were withdrawn, but thousands of extra troops were drafted into Belfast and when the authorities thought they again had the situation under control they dismissed Constable Barrett from the force and transferred his mutinous colleagues to remote outposts in the south and west of Ireland. Nonetheless, as a report issued a year later showed, the government was compelled to improve pay and conditions of service in the RIC.

Meanwhile, in another attempt to provoke the sectarian violence that Larkin had so far successfully prevented, the authorities stationed the extra troops in the Catholic parts of West Belfast, concentrating them on the Falls Road and the Grosvenor Road especially. The plan, it seems, was to provoke clashes between the Catholics and the soldiers, and the soldiers, acting no doubt under orders, did what they could to bring about such clashes. They cordoned off the working-class streets in the lower Falls, then stopped, questioned and searched everyone who passed.

This led, during the second week in August, to demonstrations against the troops, then to rioting, and eventually to bloodshed and death. On the evening of 12 August, during a riot that lasted for five hours, the troops fired on a mob of Catholics who had gathered on Grosvenor Road. In that shooting two people were killed and many others seriously wounded.

Larkin, who was on the Falls Road during these disturbances, along with other local Labour leaders, denounced the presence of troops in the Catholic districts when, he said, the strike about which they were all supposed to be concerned was taking place in another part of the town. But the Unionist newspapers, still trying to stir sectarian feelings, reported that 'Nationalist Riots' had broken out, that the soldiers had given 'splendid service,' and that Larkin's presence in Belfast was not in connection with trade unionism at all but was "part of a conspiracy against the Unionist cause in Ireland."

With the shootings the Belfast strike became national news in Britain. Some of the British trade union leaders were alarmed. They feared that the strike would develop into revolution and so, led by James Sexton, several of them hurried over to Belfast in order to get the strikers back to work as quickly as possible—and seemingly under any sort of settlement. Sexton and his friends ignored Larkin when they started talks with the employers. In September they claimed that the strike had been settled, but a month later Larkin told Belfast Trades Council that there had been no settlement and that the men were forced back by the union refusing to continue paying them strike money.

The terms that Sexton and the shipping bosses agreed on were that the carters and coal-fillers got wage increases but that the employers would have the right to employ non-union labour, if they so wished. That was on 28 August. A few days later the dockers, who got neither an increase nor protection for union members, also capitulated and told their employers, the Belfast Steamship Company, that they were very sorry for what they had done. They also promised, if reinstated in their jobs, to work with anyone the company chose to employ.

And so it seems that Larkin achieved little in Belfast; but that would not be true. Michael McKeown, who became secretary of the Dock Labourers' Union in Belfast, said soon after the strike ended that "there had never been a workers' movement in Ireland or in the whole of the United Kingdom that had made such progress as the dockers' union had done in Belfast in 1907."

If there was one part of Ireland where the workers were treated with inhumanity [said McKeown] it was along the docks of Belfast and for many years they had yearned for the day when that state of affairs would be changed. They waited till the harvest was ripe and a reaper was sent in the person of James Larkin.

Even Sexton admitted that Larkin "did so rouse the public opinion of Ireland that matters were much easier for those who took up the conflict after he had retired from it. . . ." Sexton also stated that:

Only a man of outstanding force of character could bring the police out on strike at Belfast and so cement the religious factions of Shankill and Falls Road that they joined in one harmonious procession, with bonfires blazing all over the city.

After the Belfast strike Larkin was kept busy for the next year organising branches of the Dock Labourers' Union in the main ports along the eastern coast of Ireland. In December 1907 he was called to Newry and Warrenpoint where the local shipping employers were trying hard to break a strike of the dockers. The employers' method, as usual, was to bring in non-union labour. A few months after this Larkin went to Cork where the dockers, though not at first members of the union, were involved in a dispute with the Cork Steam Packet Company.

This company, in what must have been a very expensive drive against the strikers, offered to pay blacklegs as much as thirty shillings a week, with lodgings and food thrown in, and free liquor. The regular dockers employed by the company got twenty-two shillings a week with, of course, none of the extras which the blacklegs were offered.

Despite his success in organising the Cork dockers, Larkin was later accused of misappropriating money which they had given him as their contributions to the NUDL. For this he stood trial, in 1910, and was sentenced by Judge Boyd to a year in prison with hard labour. But the Dublin Trades Council raised a petition which they presented to Lord Aberdeen, the Viceroy of Ireland. The petition succeeded and Larkin was released on 1 October, after having served three months of his sentence.

James Sexton, who was then bitterly antagonistic to Larkin and who had urged the Executive Council of the NUDL to institute proceedings over the money, gave evidence at the trial. He swore that so far as his knowledge went there had never been a branch of the NUDL in Cork. He later alleged that Larkin was released from prison because he had influential friends in Dublin Castle.

Lord Aberdeen, it is true, was a liberal and tolerant gentleman and, it has been said, "was not unimpressed by the work which Larkin was engaged in." Nonetheless, it is not easy to see what influence a trade union leader whose main achievements, since his coming to Ireland in 1907, had consisted of winning strikes and organising the unskilled would have in the circles of the Viceroy. Those people who had somewhat more sympathy for Larkin than Sexton was capable of showing believed, that if there had not been an actual miscarriage of justice in the first instance, the sentence imposed by Judge Boyd was at the very least disproportionate to the offence. The *Freeman's Journal* (3 October 1910) commented:

The circumstances under which Mr. Larkin was convicted and sentenced, in June last, are still fresh in the memory of that part of the public who take an interest in Labour disputes and their consequences, and the announcement that he will be released on October 1st causes no surprise because it was strongly felt by the public at the time of the trial that although technically he had broken the law he had been guilty of no moral turpitude, that the sentence was altogether disproportionate to the offence, and that, in fact, it ought not be allowed to stand.

William O'Brien, a union leader, who had plenty of trouble with Jim Larkin in later years, believed that "most people who were not prejudiced against Larkin took the view that it was rather a muddle on his part than anything illegal." Probably Larkin was, like so many other people, somewhat careless about keeping records of money received and paid out. Sexton's view was that "financially Larkin had the lives of nine cats and he lived all of them—most of 'em twice. He would order a strike as casually as he would ask for bacon and eggs for his breakfast, trusting to luck for the funds, even if he hadn't a copper at his command."

In November 1908 Larkin was in Derry, on union work, when he received word that the carters of Dublin were on strike and needed his help. The Dublin carters were already members of the NUDL, yet Sexton and his colleagues of the Executive Council refused to support them, and they told Larkin they would take no responsibility for the Dublin strike. So Larkin acted alone. He hurried to Dublin and was soon addressing meetings of the carters along the dockside.

For this 'breach of union discipline' Larkin was suspended from his job as NUDL organiser in Ireland, and soon after that Sexton persuaded the Executive Council to dismiss him altogether. Larkin's dismissal led to the formation of the Irish Transport Workers' Union, an organisation that was to change the course of Irish Labour history and to become one of the foremost trade unions in the world.

The ITGWU began in humble surroundings on 4 January 1909; its first central office was a bare room in a tenement house in Townsend Street, Dublin, furnished with nothing more than "a table, a couple of chairs, two empty bottles." The men who formed the union, the dockers and carters of Dublin, were dissatisfied with the generally compromising policy of the NUDL leaders. They wanted a union that would be completely free of cross-channel control and that would not shrink from militant action when such action was justified.

Among the founders of the new union was William O'Brien who had been associated with James Connolly since the early days of the Irish Socialist Republican Party in 1896. He was later to replace Larkin as general secretary.

The trade union movement, in Britain and in Ireland, was in the early 1900s influenced by syndicalist movements such as the American-based Industrial Workers of the World and by the philosophy which taught that all workers should belong to one union and that this union, being the homogeneous force of the working class, could change society from capitalism to socialism.

Syndicalism, as this philosophy was called, claimed many followers among the younger trade union leaders on both sides of the Atlantic. In Britain one of the leading syndicalists was Tom Mann. In the USA, when the ITGWU was founded, James Connolly was an organiser for the IWW and a confirmed syndicalist.

The influence of the syndicalist philosophy has declined considerably since those days, yet some traces of it can still be seen in industrial unionism, that particular form of trade unionism which holds that there should be only one union for each industry and that all workers in each particular industry, irrespective of their skill or status, should be in that one union.

This form of trade unionism prevails in the communist countries, in Western Germany, in Sweden, to some degree in the USA and to a much lesser extent in Britain. The industrial unions should not be confused, however, with the general unions. The general unions aim to organise workers in as many industries as possible, irrespective of their status or skill. The ITGWU today is a general rather than an industrial union. It has many trade sections and has members in a vast number of industries and occupations.

11

DUBLIN 1913

THE Irish Transport Workers' Union got many opportunities to prove its militancy during the years from 1909 until the outbreak of the First World War in 1914. Those were years of widespread labour unrest. There were many strikes, several of them prolonged and most of them about wages and union recognition, throughout Britain and Ireland.

Yet that was a time, as G. D. H. Cole has pointed out in his book, *The Common People*, when Britain dominated the world and when British exports were increasing every year much faster than imports. What is nowadays called the balance-of-payments problem did not exist. But this did not mean that the working people were better off; it merely meant that the upper classes got richer.

By 1910, when the period of labour unrest began, the workers were actually worse off than they had been in the mid-1890s. Prices had risen; the value of their money-wages had fallen. Inflation, in other words, had reduced their standard of living. Their money bought less bread, meat, sugar and other basic necessities.

At the same time unemployment was increasing. In 1907 something like 4 per cent of the industrial labour force was out of work; in 1910 the unemployment figure was 8 per cent. "The labour unrest of 1910 and the following years," wrote Cole, "had behind it the full force of the bread and butter argument."

The conditions under which the poorer people lived in the city of Dublin were worse than the conditions in most other cities, not only in the United Kingdom but in Europe. Nearly one-third of Dublin's 300,000 citizens lived in tumbledown tenements and slums, many of which had been condemned not merely as being unfit for human habitation but of being incapable of ever being made fit. Most of the slum-dwelling families lived in one room; their average income, if they were the families of unskilled labourers, was rarely more than 20 shillings a week.

In the Republican newspaper, *Irish Freedom*, Padraig Pearse wrote that "the tenement houses of Dublin are so rotten that now and then they collapse, and if the inhabitants collect in the streets to discuss matters the police baton them." So what is today called 'Rachmanism' was rampant in Dublin in 1913. It was supported by all the force of the Dublin Metropolitan Police, the Royal Irish Constabulary, Dublin Castle and the British army.

While these conditions prevailed, while real wages fell in value and unemployment increased, the profits of industry rose and more capital accumulated in the hands of financiers, manufacturers and businessmen. Most of this new capital was, however, invested abroad and very little of it in Britain or Ireland. Ireland could not, therefore, escape the effects of the labour unrest.

There was a general strike of Irish railway workers in 1911. During that same year the Dublin bakers went on strike because labour-saving ovens had been installed in the bakehouses of Johnston, Mooney and O'Brien Ltd. There was a strike of sailors. There were strikes in Cork, Dublin, Sligo, Wexford and elsewhere. These disputes enhanced the standing of the Irish Transport Workers' Union. By 1910 the union had 3,000 members and had been accepted into affiliation with the Irish TUC. Larkin's imprisonment, far from doing the union harm, increased the membership still further.

The Irish employers reacted, as they had reacted in Belfast in 1907, by trying to smash the union. Some of them like William Martin Murphy, the Dublin financier, newspaper proprietor and public transport tycoon, became personally antagonistic to Larkin. Murphy denounced the Irish Transport Workers' Union as a menace to all trade organisations.

The employers feared most of all the sympathetic strike tactics which Larkin was using everywhere with great effect. They formed employers' federations in Dublin and Cork to fight against him. Larkin, for his part, lampooned and lacerated the employers, the Castle, and the police in his weekly paper, *The Irish Worker*. The first issue of this paper appeared in June 1911 and the last when the British Government suppressed it during the first weeks of the 1914–18 War.

When the union formed a branch in Cork, in 1909, the local employers tried to undermine it by supporting a rival organisation of blacklegs. In Belfast the employers had rather less trouble; there the traditional hostility between Catholics and Protestants prevented the progress of the Belfast branch. It was not until 1911 when James Connolly was posted as organiser in Belfast that the union became firmly established in the North.

Meanwhile the Dublin employers, led and inspired by Murphy, were preparing a major assault. The attack came in the summer of 1913 in the form of the Great Dublin Lock-Out. This was the bitterest struggle between capital and labour in the whole history of Ireland.

During the first six months of 1913 there were several minor strikes in Dublin, in all of which the Irish Transport Workers' Union was involved. The strikes first affected the dockers, who refused to work with non-unionists; then the men in the building trades, and then the clerks and carters. Meanwhile Larkin was organising incessantly. He called sympathetic strikes when he thought them justified on the grounds that the workers in all industries, and in all unions, should stand together.

And he kept pointing out that, from the unions' point of view, there were two black spots in Dublin. One of these was Arthur Guinness's brewery; the other was the Dublin United Tramways Co. which was owned and operated by Murphy.

Little could be done about the brewery where the workers were fairly well treated and did not feel the need to belong to a trade union. The Dublin trams, in fact all the enterprises controlled by Murphy, presented a different problem. They were all non-union, though for several weeks before August Larkin and his colleagues had been enrolling the tramwaymen and the workers in the despatch department of Murphy's newspaper, the *Irish Independent*.

This alarmed Murphy. In mid-August he moved into an attacking position. He called a meeting of all his employees in the despatch department and ordered them to leave the union if they were already members and not to join if asked to do so. On 19 August he dismissed those workers who disobeyed this order. Larkin immediately organised sympathetic action. The newsboys on Dublin's streets refused to sell the *Irish Independent*;

the workers in Easons, the main wholesale distributors, came out on strike.

A week later, on Tuesday 26 August, the tram crews stopped work and left their vehicles abandoned on the streets. Non-union crews were immediately engaged, and drove the trams under the protection of the Dublin Metropolitan Police. Murphy had already been assured by Dublin Castle that not only the DMP but also the Royal Irish Constabulary and, if need be, the British army, would be called in to help him in the fight against what the authorities referred to as 'Larkinism.'

The DMP were very active. On Tuesday at a strike meeting in Beresford Place they arrested Larkin and four of his leading colleagues and charged them all with 'seditious libel.' The five union leaders were also accused, in a remarkable and almost bloodthirsty indictment, "of seditious conspiracy, of disturbing the peace and raising discontent and hatred among certain classes of His Majesty's subjects, of inciting hatred and contempt of the government, and of inciting murder."

The union leaders appeared before a magistrate by name of Swifte but were released on bail pending trial. That same morning Swifte issued a proclamation, at the request of the DMP, banning a meeting which Larkin intended to hold in O'Connell Street on Sunday 31 August. The proclamation stated that the proposed meeting was unlawful and seditious and "would cause terror and alarm to and dissension among His Majesty's subjects."

Larkin's reply was to burn a copy of the proclamation at another meeting in Beresford Place and to declare that come what may he would speak at the meeting in O'Connell Street on Sunday.

These are the events that led to what is known in Irish labour history as Bloody Sunday 1913. And it was afterwards revealed that Swifte the magistrate was quite a large shareholder in Murphy's tramway business.

On Friday and Saturday the police attacked groups of union members assembled on Eden Quay and within the vicinity of Liberty Hall, the union headquarters. The union members, it is true, had been trying to stop the trams that were manned by blackleg crews. This brought "savage counter-attacks from foot and mounted police. . . . Hundreds of union members were injured, scores taken to hospital in ambulances and many arrested. Thirty policemen were hospital cases."

James Nolan, a young member of the union, was beaten so savagely by the police that his skull was smashed in. He died

on Sunday morning; and Sean O'Casey, who was also a member
of the union, went to see the corpse laid out in its coffin. In
Drums Under the Window O'Casey described what he saw:

> There he was asprawl under a snowy sheet, looking like a mask
> on a totem pole, one eye gone, the other askew, the nose cracked at
> the bridge and bent sideways; the forehead and one cheek royal
> purple: from a distance it looked like a fading iris on a wide patch
> of snow. The mighty baton!

Two other workers who lost their lives in 1913 were John
Byrne, who was also beaten by the police, and Alice Brady, a
young girl who was shot dead by an armed blackleg on one of
the trams. O'Casey stood on the pavement in O'Connell Street,
among the crowd of people who watched the funerals go by:

> Here it comes, the Dead March in Saul, flooding the street, and
> flowing into the windows of the street's richest buildings, followed
> by the bannered Labour unions, the colours sobered by cordons of
> crepe, a host of sodden grey following a murdered comrade.

At midday on Sunday 31 August, O'Connell Street was filled
with people; thousands of them came up from the docks and
slums and alleyways of the city because Larkin had promised
that he would be there to speak. At one o'clock precisely,
disguised as an elderly deaf clergyman, he stepped out of a
carriage and entered the Imperial Hotel. A few minutes later
he had cast off his disguise and was addressing the crowd from
a balcony on the second floor of the hotel.

His appearance on the balcony was almost a signal for the
police to act. Several constables rushed into the hotel and
arrested Larkin. Outside, hundreds of other constables, some
mounted and some on foot, charged the crowd. O'Casey was
one of the people who fled from this attack, but hundreds of
people could not escape and "the scene of the disturbances," it
was reported, "was strewn like a battlefield with the bodies of
injured people, many of them with their faces covered in blood
and their bodies writhing in agony."

The police themselves did not escape unhurt. Almost 200 of
them, it was reported, were injured when the crowd fought back.
How many civilians suffered was never known but next day the
newspapers reported hundreds injured on both sides. Headlines
announced: Bloodshed in Dublin; Hospitals Overcrowded;
Fierce Baton Charges, etc.

The newspapers also reported that Larkin had been arrested
and was being held in custody, and that James Connolly, who

had been recalled from Belfast to help in Dublin, was also in jail. The leadership in the struggle then passed to William O'Brien and P. T. Daly. They immediately sent a deputation to Manchester to seek the help of the British TUC.

The TUC leaders may not have been as enthusiastic as the Dublin leaders would have hoped but they did raise a substantially large sum of money for the men whom Murphy and his colleagues had turned out of their employment. Altogether the total amount raised by the TUC, subscribed by unions like the Miners' Federation of Great Britain, and collected by the socialist newspapers was about £150,000.

The unions in Dublin needed this money because the employers were determined to wage a long and bitter struggle against the ITGWU. And with Larkin and Connolly both locked in jail some of the smaller employers became more aggressive. George N. Jacob closed his biscuit factory. The Dublin Coal Merchants' Association locked out all their delivery men.

Then, on Wednesday 3 September, some 400 employers, described as "the largest and most representative body of Dublin merchants, manufacturers and traders" ever to meet in the city, decided, under the chairmanship of Murphy himself, "not to employ any persons who continue to be members of the Irish Transport and General Workers' Union."

They also decided that "any person refusing to carry out our lawful and reasonable instructions or the instructions of those placed over them" would be instantly dismissed no matter to what trade union they belonged.

Three days later these employers attempted to impose a non-union contract upon their employees. Every worker in their employment was ordered to resign his membership of the Irish Transport and General Workers' Union or, if he was not already a member, to give an undertaking not to join the union or support it in any way. This document was to be signed by each employee and signed also by a witness.

At the end of September, a Court of Inquiry which had been set up by the Board of Trade to investigate the causes of the Dublin dispute came to the conclusion that:

This document imposed upon the signatories conditions which are contrary to individual liberty, and which no workman or body of workmen could reasonably be expected to accept.

The chairman of the court of inquiry was Sir George Askwith, a well-known and respected arbitrator in trade disputes, yet the Dublin employers refused to accept either the court's findings or its recommendations. By then, with all the employers united behind Murphy, something like 20,000 workmen had been put out of their jobs. Altogether when the families of these workmen were included a total of 100,000 people in the city of Dublin was being denied the right to earn a livelihood.

The suffering of these people and the stubborn refusal of the employers to accept the court's findings prompted the poet AE (George Russell) to write a scathing letter to the *Irish Times*. That letter is one of the famous documents of the 1913 Dublin Lock-Out. In it Russell accused the employers of having "determined deliberately, in cold anger, to starve out one-third of the population of this city, to break the manhood of the men by the sight of the suffering of their wives and the hunger of their children."

Larkin fought with great courage during the dispute; even those men who were later to be among his enemies and critics in the Irish Labour movement admitted that. He was released from jail on £100 bail and appeared as the workers' attorney at the court of inquiry. There he cross-examined Murphy and engaged in verbal combat with Tim Healy, a Nationalist politician, later Governor-General of the Irish Free State, and one of the most virulent advocates in the Irish courts.

When the employers refused to accept the recommendations of the court of inquiry public opinion turned against them, and even the London *Times* said it was time W. M. Murphy and his friends "learned their lesson." The trade union movement in Britain was completely behind Larkin and the Dublin workers.

Larkin then embarked on a campaign of meetings throughout Britain so that the support of the trade unions there could be effectively mobilised. Wherever he went he called on the British workers to organise sympathetic strikes, to refuse to handle what he called 'tainted goods' and to prevent blacklegs being sent to Dublin. This campaign infuriated the top trade union leaders in Britain, especially as Larkin, whose speeches usually inspired men to action, succeeded in getting strikes started in Liverpool, Manchester and Birmingham.

The British union leaders had no intention of getting their unions involved in what could easily have become a general strike in all industries. Their view was that so long as money was being collected and sent to Dublin there was no need for the British workers to be further involved.

And so some of the TUC leaders began to denounce Larkin as an irresponsible agitator. In an effort to counteract the effects of his strike-promoting campaign in Britain they sent a delegation to Dublin, hoping to make contact with the employers and to bring the dispute there to an end. Murphy and the other employers met the delegation, discussed the dispute with them, but, like the Belfast employers in 1907, refused to have anything to do with Larkin or to recognise the Irish Transport Workers' Union.

Meanwhile the Dublin dispute had become international news. V. I. Lenin, the leader of the Russian Bolsheviks, had been studying events in Ireland and in one of his pamphlets he wrote:

> The Irish proletariat that is awakening to class consciousness has found a talented leader in the person of Comrade Larkin, the secretary of the Irish Transport Workers' Union. Possessing remarkable oratorical talent, a man of seething Irish energy, Larkin has performed miracles among the unskilled.

Larkin and Lenin never met, for by the time Larkin made contact with the Communist International and was invited to Moscow Lenin was dead.

When the British trade union leaders refused to involve their members in the Dublin dispute Larkin's denunciations of them became increasingly furious. Indeed one of the least offensive things he said about them was that they were "about as useful as mummies in a museum." At other times he described them as 'serpents.' They had "neither a soul to be saved nor a body to be kicked."

Among the British Labour leaders who felt the lash of his bitter tongue were Ramsey McDonald, J. H. Thomas and Philip Snowden. Less than twenty years after 1913 Larkin was to see these men betray the Labour movement in its hour of greatest need, desert the trade unions, and become members of a Tory-controlled Cabinet in London. In 1935 Thomas was disgraced and kicked out of politics for betraying the secrets of the British budget.

At one stage in 1913 Larkin approved a scheme to evacuate some of the locked-out workers' children to England, where they would be properly housed and fed for the duration of the dispute. Hundreds of working-class families in the North of England, many of them probably Irish Catholic families, had agreed to take the children. But when news of this scheme reached Dr. William Walsh, the Catholic Archbishop of Dublin, he became very angry and immediately denounced Larkin and the two women social workers, Dora Montefiori and Lucille Rand, who were to be responsible for taking the children to England. Dr. Walsh said in a letter to the newspapers that any mothers who allowed their children to be taken "to a strange land without security of any kind" were not worthy to be called 'Catholic mothers.'

And then followed one of the most distressing incidents in the whole dispute. Young priests of the Dublin diocese acting on the word of their Archbishop organised bands of parents, held meetings on the Dublin and Dun Laoghaire quaysides and prevented the children from going on board the steamships to England. The clergy ignored the humanitarian motives of Mrs. Montefiori and Mrs. Rand and saw the scheme merely as an attempt to undermine the faith of the children and to place them in the homes of 'godless English socialists.'

The two ladies were arrested and charged with kidnapping; but they were soon set free because it was quite obvious that none of the children was being sent or could have been sent to England without the willing consent of their parents.

And there was no doubt that the children, as well as their parents, were starving. The struggle with Murphy had been going on for two months. Relief money, substantial though it may have seemed in the aggregate, was meagre when divided among the families of the men on the streets. In an effort to alleviate the hardship, Liberty Hall, headquarters of the union, opened a food depot where the Countess Markievicz and her assistants did their best to feed the people, and there was great joy in Liberty Hall when two ships, laden with food and supplies and sent by the co-operative societies in Britain, arrived in Dublin port.

Larkin's bail expired at the end of October. He stood trial on the original charge of incitement to disorder, was found guilty and sentenced to seven months without hard labour. But he served only two weeks of this sentence. A campaign of meetings in Britain, addressed by Bernard Shaw, W. B. Yeats, George Russell, George Lansbury, Keir Hardie and other well-known people, roused public opinion and forced the Government to release Larkin. The Government at that time lost two by-elections to the Tories, and one of the explanations for these defeats, said Lloyd George, was 'Jim Larkin.'

At that time Ireland was on the verge of a Unionist rebellion aganst Home Rule. In the North Edward Carson had organised and was preparing to arm an illegal army, the Ulster Volunteer Force. In the South on 25 November 1913, The O'Rahilly, Bulmer Hobson, Eoin MacNeill, Sean MacDiarmada, Padraig Pearse and other Nationalists and republicans formed the Irish Volunteers. About a month earlier the Irish Citizen Army had come into being. Organised and equipped by Connolly, trained and drilled by Jack White, an ex-officer of the British army and son of Field-Marshal White, the ICA went to the protection of the Dublin workers in 1913 when they were attacked by the police. Three years later, in 1916, the Citizen Army joined with the Irish Volunteers and took part in the Easter Rising.

The formation of the ICA was, perhaps, the one real lasting outcome of the 1913 Lock-Out, because in the end neither Murphy nor Larkin won. Archbishop Walsh called a conciliation conference in Dublin; the TUC held a special delegate conference in London, but no settlement was ever reached. The employers eventually agreed to re-employ those workers who applied for jobs, provided there were jobs for them. At the same time they did not agree to recognise the Irish Transport Workers' Union. In his summing up of the dispute James Connolly wrote:

The battle was a drawn battle. The employers, despite their Napoleonic plan of campaign, and their more than Napoleonic ruthlessness and unscrupulous use of foul means, were unable to carry on their business without men and women who remained loyal to the union. The workers were unable to force the employers to a formal recognition of the union, and to give preference to organised labour.

By January 1914 the Dublin dispute was over. Six months later Larkin went to the United States of America on a lecture tour to raise money for the union. He did not return to Ireland until 1923 and by then he found that the leadership of the union had passed into the hands of other men.

Larkin's main activity during his exile in the USA was campaigning against the 1914–18 war and, in later years, promoting socialism and support for the Soviet Union. But after the Bolshevik Revolution, America was swept by a fear of communism, and in 1919 Larkin, along with many other socialist agitators, was arrested on a charge of criminal anarchy. He was found guilty and sentenced to five years in Sing Sing prison.

In 1922 Governor Al Smith granted Larkin a free pardon, stating as he granted the pardon that he thought Larkin's case was "a political case where a man had been punished for the statement of his beliefs." Governor Smith then spelt out one of the fundamental safeguards that all people holding minority and unpopular opinion are entitled to in democratic society:

Political progress results from the clash of conflicting opinions. The public assertion of an erroneous doctrine is perhaps the surest way to disclose the error and make it evident to the electorate. And it is a distinct disservice to the state to impose, for the utterance of a misguided opinion, such extreme punishment as may tend to deter, in proper cases, that full and free discussion of political issues which is a fundamental of democracy.

When Larkin reached Ireland he was greeted by great numbers of workers and former comrades but he soon found that he just could not take up where he had left off in 1914. The Executive Council of the Irish Transport and General Workers' Union refused to reinstate him in the position of general secretary. He quarrelled with his former colleagues. There was bad feeling on both sides and eventually some members of the union broke away under his leadership to form the Workers' Union of Ireland.

The WUI was, however, one of many new Irish unions which were set up after the partition of Ireland. Some of these unions took the view that the Irish Labour movement should be organisationally independent of the British trade unions. Thus began a conflict between British-based unions and Irish-based unions that was later to have serious consequences.

12

POGROMS AND POVERTY

WHEN Connolly and Captain White created the Irish Citizen Army, which was an avowedly socialist and revolutionary movement, the Tory politicians and Orangemen who dominated Belfast felt there was urgent need for an organisation that would keep Protestant workers apart from Catholics, promote sectarianism within the trade unions, and counteract the influence of the socialists. They had learned, from the strike of 1907, that even the Orange Order, effective though it was in fomenting strife and bigotry, could be undermined by a united Labour movement.

And so they set up an organisation to which they gave the name Ulster Unionist-Labour Association and which, they suggested, would "demonstrate the identity of working men with Unionism."

The Unionist-Labour Association has remained to the present day, but it has not been notably successful. One Unionist apologist, J. R. Sayers, regretted that the association had "not influenced the party councils" and that William Grant, who became a Northern Ireland Cabinet Minister, was "the last to speak with authority for those who are trade unionists as well as Unionists."

Nonetheless the principle that Labour in Ulster should be pro-British has been accepted beyond the ranks of Unionist Labour and has exerted a tragic influence on the Labour Party and on many of the trade unions in Northern Ireland.

It is not certain when the Ulster Unionist-Labour Association started. The official records of the Unionist Party give the inaugural date as June 1918, a few months before the end of the First World War, but Clarkson, in his *Labour and Nationalism in Ireland,* traces the origins of the movement to April 1914. He names the three original or 'charter' members as Edward Carson, the Unionist leader; J. M. Andrews, a large linen employer who in 1940 was to become Prime Minister of Northern Ireland; and William Grant, who was prominent in the Orange Order and in the Unionist Party and chairman of the Belfast branch of the shipwrights' union.

Fr. John Hassan, a Catholic priest who wrote under the pseudonym of 'G. B. Kenna,' compiled a day-by-day account of the dreadful religious pogroms that swept through Belfast from July 1920 until August 1922. In his book he stated that the political activities of the Ulster Unionist-Labour Association "were completely successful in driving a solid wedge between the Protestant and Catholic workers, and in fostering among the former a spirit which was soon to show itself in the shipyard pogrom."

Hassan noted that, in 1919, "there had been growing up, steadily and unobtrusively, a feeling of the solidarity of labour, and a tendency to forget the differences of Orange and Green in attempts to achieve objects of common interest to workers in Belfast, irrespective of creed or politics." He stated that "this movement culminated in the 44-hour strike when shipyard workers, under the chairmanship of a Catholic trade unionist, carried the struggle almost to victory."

The 44-hour strike started on Clydeside where the workers in engineering and shipbuilding demanded a reduction in the working week, which had been 54 hours since 1878. The demands of the workers were expressed at mass meetings in Glasgow. There was violence when the police attacked 50,000 Scottish trade unionists who had assembled in St. George's Square.

After that the agitation for the shorter working week spread to London, Edinburgh, Leith and Belfast. It ended with the unions accepting a 47-hour week. In the same year, 1919, the

Amalgamated Society of Engineers won an extra five shillings a week for skilled men employed in the Belfast shipyards and marine engineering plants.

Unionist politicians in Belfast, as well as the owners of the Belfast shipyards, were, according to Hassan, "aghast at this manifest unity of Catholics and Protestants, and were not long in setting to work to make sure that never again should such a situation be allowed to develop."

At the Orange demonstrations on 12 July 1920 Edward Carson told the Protestants who worked in the shipyards that "they were in imminent danger from Sinn Fein, that he was losing hope of the British Government being able to defend them, and that they must do something to protect themselves." He said that he was "sick of mere words and that what he wanted was action."

The Unionist newspapers published every word of Carson's speech, and, for the whole week that followed, printed letters from readers who alleged that "Roman Catholics, Nationalists and Sinn Feiners were pouring into the province of Ulster and threatening to drive out the Protestants." Like Carson, the writers of these letters demanded action and an end to words and empty protestations of loyalty.

In response to these calls for action the Belfast Protestant Association, an extreme loyalist organisation, printed and posted placards throughout the Queen's Island, calling all "Unionist and Protestant workers" to a lunchtime meeting. At that meeting firearms were brandished, and it was resolved that "all Roman Catholics, Sinn Feiners and Nationalists" as well as "all un-reliable Protestants and socialists" should be driven from the shipyards. Hassan, who lived in the centre of Belfast at the time, recorded what happened:

Immediately after the meeting a violent onslaught was made upon the Catholic employees as well as on a dozen or so Protestants who refused to bow the knee to Carson. They were peremptorily ordered to clear out. Being in a minority of one to six they could not put up a fight with any hope of success. Those who could get quietly away accepted the inevitable. Many came in for various kinds of attack. Hundreds were surrounded and kicked. Several were thrown into water, twenty-five feet deep, and pelted with bolts and other missiles as they struggled for life. Even according to the Orange press—which, as we shall see, has hardly admitted any Orange delinquencies—men swimming from their pursuers were pelted back from the opposite bank, and one man had to swim for safety to Sydenham, a mile distant. No one was killed outright, but nearly a score of very seriously injured were conveyed to hospital, and a large number of others badly hurt were treated at home. . . . When it was all over, and the Catholics cleared out, a force of military arrived, and the pogromists, as the *Northern Whig* informs us, received the forces of the law with cheers and the singing of loyal choruses.

Further details of what happened were given by a representative of the Belfast Expelled Workers to the annual conference of the Irish TUC on 4 August. He said that:

On July 21 men armed with sledge hammers and other weapons swooped down on the Catholic workers in the shipyards, and did not even give them a chance for their lives. . . . The gates were smashed down with sledges, the vests and shirts of those at work were torn open to see were the men wearing any Catholic emblems, and then woe betide the man who was. One man was set upon, thrown into the dock, had to swim the Musgrave Channel, and having been pelted with rivets had to swim two or three miles, to emerge in streams of blood and rush to the police in a nude state.

The persecution and intimidation of Catholics took place in other industries besides the shipyards. Thousands of Catholic working people, men and women, were driven from the textile factories, from engineering firms, from building sites, and from their own homes if they were unfortunate enough to live in predominantly Protestant districts.

In August 1920 a delegation from the Executive Council of the Amalgamated Society of Carpenters and Joiners, which was concerned about the persecution of its Catholic members, arrived in Belfast and met the heads of the two local shipbuilding firms, Harland and Wolff Ltd., and Workman Clarke Ltd. But when the delegates tried to arrange a mass meeting of ASC&J members the military chiefs, acting on the advice of the Unionist politicians, intervened and banned the meeting. A few weeks later, 21 September, the Executive Council of the Carpenters' Union ordered all its Belfast members not to work for firms from which Catholic members of the union had been evicted. The circular issued by the union stated:

In consequence of the serious disturbances in Belfast District, causing the expulsion of several hundred members of our society from the shipyards, where they were peacefully earning their livelihood, you are hereby informed that you must not accept employment from, or remain in the employment of, the following firms:
Messrs. Harland and Wolff, Shipbuilders,
Messrs. Workman and Clarke,
Messrs. McLaughlin and Harvey, Housebuilders,
Messrs. Coombe, Barbour, Fairbairn, and Lawson, Engineers,
Messrs. Musgrave and Company Limited, Engineers,

Messrs. Davidson and Company Limited,
Messrs. The Sirocco Works, Belfast,
Messrs. James Mackie and Company,
after 25th September 1920. Any member remaining in the employment
of these firms after the above date will be expelled from our society. . . .

Only 600 members obeyed the directive; 2,000 remained in
their jobs and were, consequently, expelled from the society.

The Queen's Island has been notorious for generations as
a place where the Protestant workers were likely in times of
communal unrest to turn violently against their Catholic work-
mates. The original shipbuilding labour force had been brought
from Clydeside and Tyneside by Edward Harland when he took
over and expanded the industry in the early 1850s. And from
the beginning these migrants earned the reputation of being
violent bigots. They were active in all the sectarian riots that
shook Belfast during the nineteenth century. During the Home
Rule riots of 1886 they attacked and drove the Catholics out
of Queen's Island and were the cause, on that occasion, of one
young workman being drowned.

In April 1893, another year of Home Rule riots, the Protestant
shipyard workers again attacked the Catholics and posted
notices warning them that if they dared return to work they
would end up in the River Lagan. They stoned the policemen
and soldiers who were sent to protect the Catholics.

During those troubles the Belfast branches of the Associated
Shipwrights' Society, the Amalgamated Society of Engineers,
the Boilermakers and Iron Shipbuilders' Society, the Associated
Blacksmiths' Society, the United Patternmakers' Association,
the Amalgamated Society of Mill Sawyers and Woodcutting
Machinists, the Sailmakers' Union, the Belfast Operative House
Painters' Union, and the Tyneside National Labour Union—
all sent letters to Harland and Wolff condemning "the foul and
dastardly attacks in the Queen's Island upon our fellow-workmen and fellow-citizens." The unions also advised all the
Catholics who had fled from the shipyards to return to their
jobs as quickly as possible. The firm sent the following letter,
dated 27 April 1893, in reply to the unions' protest:

We are in receipt of your letter forming a resolution passed by
your society regarding the present differences between our workmen,
and we are very pleased at the early step you have taken to try and
rectify matters, as far as your society goes, so that the men who had
to leave their employment either through violence, threats, or fears,
may return to their usual duties. We trust that the other societies

and tradesmen in the yard may follow your example, when peace will no doubt be restored and we will be able to go on working full-time. . . .

Two days before they sent out the letter to the unions the firm had posted a notice throughout the works which stated that:

In consequence of the continued disturbance at meal times in these works, they will for the present not be open until 8.30 a.m. when those who wish to start must have their breakfast taken. We trust that no further disturbances will take place, as we shall be sorry to adopt more severe measures; and we may point out to those of our men who are for the cause of the Union that nothing could be more injurious to it than the proceedings which have taken place at these works.

By "the cause of the Union," the firm meant, of course, the political union with Britain, not the trade union. The two heads of the firm, Edward Harland and G. W. Wolff, were both prominent Unionist politicians. In 1893 Wolff was a Unionist MP. Harland had been Unionist Mayor of Belfast in 1886.

Harland and Wolff's shipyard was not the only place where, in 1893, workers were terrorised because of their religion or their political outlook. According to evidence which the Catholic Committee in Belfast presented to the British Government, Catholic women employed in at least eighteen of Belfast's textile factories were violently attacked by Protestants. They were set upon by women "wielding knives and pickers" in Boyd's mill on Peter's Hill. They were driven out of Ewart's finishing factory in Bedford Street and out of Ewart's spinning mill on Crumlin Road. They were beaten in Valentine's factory while two policemen stood by and did not interfere.

Neither the protests of the unions nor the posters put up by the management of Harland and Wolff Ltd. had any lasting effect. The Catholic workers in Queen's Island and in other Belfast firms and factories were the victims of sectarian attacks in 1898, in 1912, during the 1920-22 pogroms, in 1935, and again in 1969 and 1970. In June 1970, after a weekend of sectarian rioting in East Belfast, the 500 Catholics employed in Queen's Island were threatened and forced to leave their jobs.

And once again the trade unions, acting together as the Confederation of Shipbuilding and Engineering Unions, took action to get the Catholics reinstated. At the same time the management of Harland and Wolff, in an attempt to put an end to threats and intimidation, posted a warning on all the notice boards and in prominent places throughout the 'yards:

The company are determined that all employees, irrespective of their religious beliefs, should be able to work in an atmosphere free from intimidation. Anyone, accordingly, who is subjected to any pressure whatever, and from any source within the company, should report the matter immediately to his relevant personnel office. Any employee who is proved to have used threats or intimidation against any other employee will be instantly dismissed.

The sectarian hooligans who attacked their fellow-workers in the shipyards and textile factories used the same violence against the Labour Party. William McMullen, a shipyard worker who helped Jim Larkin during the 1907 carters' strike and who was eventually to become National President of the Irish Transport and General Workers' Union, recalled how, during an election campaign, in 1921, an Orange mob from Queen's Island invaded a Labour meeting in Belfast's Ulster Hall and caused so much trouble that the socialist speakers had to be escorted home under police protection. James Craig, who was then the leader of the Unionist Party, congratulated the shipyardmen for breaking up the Labour meeting. He sent them a telegram from London, expressing his thanks.

During the early 1920s there was little effective trade union activity in the six counties of Northern Ireland. Unemployment was high. In fact the total number of 'insured workers' who were out of work all over Ireland in December 1921 was 114,000, along with another 20,000 casual workers who were employed for only a few hours each week. And this total did not include uninsured workers such as domestic servants, farm labourers etc. for whom the rate of unemployment was not then recorded. Twenty-six per cent of all Ireland's industrial workers were unemployed in 1921, while another 4 per cent were on short time. The comparative figures for Britain were 15.7 per cent unemployed and 2.3 per cent on short time. Unemployment in the Six Counties was 24 per cent in 1925. It went up to nearly 30 per cent between 1930 and 1938.

While civil war raged in the Irish Free State and sectarian violence was widespread in the North, the employers took advantage of their favourable position to attack the unions and cut wages. Wages in shipbuilding and engineering were slashed by as much as twenty-two shillings a week; dockers in Belfast lost three shillings a day; joiners and carpenters were threatened with a twelve-shillings reduction. And, in 1925, when unemployed men in Belfast organised a march to coincide with the opening of the Northern Ireland parliament, Dawson Bates, the Minister of Home Affairs, intervened. He banned the march and said it was an attempt to intimidate the government.

But with all the economic hardships and political coercion they had to put up with, the Protestant workers continued to vote for the Unionist Party and to follow men like Carson and James Craig. The Catholics were a lot more sensible. In 1924 they elected five Labour representatives to the Belfast Board of Poor Law Guardians, and in the 1925 general election for the Northern Ireland parliament they returned three Labour members: Jack Beattie, a shipyard blacksmith; Sam Kyle, a linen worker; and William McMullen.

Kyle and McMullen lost their seats when the Unionist Government abolished proportional representation in 1929, but Beattie remained a member of the Northern Ireland parliament until 1949, and was afterwards elected to Westminster as the Labour member for West Belfast.

The first serious attempt to change the political outlook of the Northern Protestant working man was the formation of a division of the National Council of Labour Colleges in Belfast at the beginning of 1924. The Labour Colleges movement had started in Britain a few years before the outbreak of the First World War and by 1920 was strong enough to unite all the local colleges into a national organisation, the NCLC.

In 1924 J. P. M. Millar, General Secretary of the NCLC, was invited to meet trade union leaders in Belfast and in Dublin with a view to setting up Labour colleges in both cities. The colleges were to provide courses in economics, social history, politics, trade unionism, etc., and were to be open to members of all unions that affiliated to the NCLC.

The trade unions in Belfast agreed to this scheme but in Dublin, largely because the Irish Transport and General Workers' Union and one or two other Irish unions were then considering how to develop their own educational schemes, no Labour college was formed. Millar got the impression, as he later told the Executive Council of the NCLC, that the unions in the South had "strong nationalistic feelings." In later years he often said that had the Dublin unions set up a Labour college and agreed to the appointment of an organiser for the whole of Ireland they "would have made a substantial contribution towards creating real unity between trade unionists in the North and trade unionists in the South."

At the time the Belfast Labour college was set up there was an active branch of the Workers' Educational Association in the city, but while the WEA attracted some trade unionists and members of the local Labour parties to its courses, it was not so clearly committed to the socialist philosophy as the NCLC. It was associated with the Extramural Department at Queen's University, Belfast, and received financial help from the government and from the local education authorities.

Through time the NCLC became the dominant educational influence within the trade unions of the North, but its influence was never strong enough to undermine the hold that Unionist politics and Orange prejudices had on the minds of the Protestant working class.

The General Strike, which started when the mineowners in Britain cut the miners' wages and which, for ten days in May 1926, brought Britain "near to revolution," did not last long enough to have any direct effect on the Irish trade unions. One reason may have been that the General Council of the British Trades Union Congress ended the strike just when it seemed that Stanley Baldwin and his Government were about to surrender.

A year later, in 1927, the British parliament passed the elaborate Trade Dispute and Trade Union Act which restricted the political rights of the unions, outlawed the sympathetic strike and made it unlawful for workers in government employment to combine with other workers. The parliament of Northern Ireland passed an identical, but separate, act. But whereas the British act was entirely repealed in 1945, parts of the Northern Ireland act are still in force.

During the 1920s many Irish trade unionists were in a revolutionary mood. Some, of course, had been members of the Irish Citizen Army and had been influenced by the socialistic philosophy of James Connolly. And Connolly, because of his part in the Easter Rising, had become a national hero, along with all the other 1916 leaders.

Countess Markievicz gave lectures on Connolly socialism in the Dublin headquarters of the republicans. Connolly's books and pamphlets were reprinted and circulated by the Irish Transport and General Workers' Union. In 1926, at the inaugural conference of the Fianna Fail Party, Eamonn de Valera said that no republican could disagree with James Connolly's principles.

In 1920, during a strike over wages, members of the ITGWU took possession of the Knocklong Creamery in Co. Limerick and established a form of workers' control. A few weeks later the miners in the Arigna Coalfield in Co. Leitrim did likewise. And in many ports around the Irish coast dockers and railwaymen refused to unload supplies and ammunition for the British forces in Ireland. On 12 April that year the Irish TUC called a general strike in support of republican political prisoners who had gone on hunger strike.

"The response was instantaneous," said Louie Bennett, Secretary of the Irish Women Workers' Union. Workers in many towns came out on strike and stayed out for three days. The prisoners were, as a consequence, unconditionally released.

Exactly two years before that, on 23 April 1918, the Irish TUC had called a one-day general strike to protest against the British Government's plan to impose conscription on Ireland. In her book, *The Irish Republic,* Dorothy McArdle wrote that:

Everywhere in Ireland, except in Belfast, shops and factories were closed and trains and trams suspended while grave and orderly throngs of people walked through the streets. No newspapers appeared in the South or West. All licensed premises were closed as were the small shops which were usually open on public holidays. In the large hotels guests were obliged to attend to their own needs. Hackney-car drivers refused to take passengers even in cases where visitors, anxious to go to the Punchestown Races, offered fares of ten pounds.

In the early Free State Dail, during the years when the elected republican deputies refused to take the Oath of Allegiance to the British Crown and were, therefore, debarred from taking their seats, the Irish Labour Party was the official Opposition. Labour eventually helped Fianna Fail to defeat the Free State Party, Cumann na nGael, and prepared the way for de Valera to become Taoiseach in 1932.

In October 1932, when the world economic crisis was at its worst with millions of people destitute in Europe and America, the working-class Catholics and Protestants of Belfast united in a protest against starvation. In that month the closing words of James Connolly's *Labour in Irish History* rang true:

. . . the pressure of a common exploitation can make enthusiastic rebels out of a Protestant working class, earnest champions of civil and religious liberty out of Catholics, and out of both a united social democracy.

In 1932 Falls Road and Shankill, West Belfast and Ballymacarrett, joined in the Out-Door-Relief Demonstrations. This movement started when 2,000 men, who were forced to work on the roads in return for relief money, went on strike. The maximum relief had been fixed by the Belfast Board of Poor Law Guardians at twenty-four shillings a week for a man, his wife and his family. Unmarried people got no relief at all; they were expected to starve, emigrate, beg, or live on their relations.

With the strike of relief workers came a rents-strike and a strike of school children. Mass meetings of people were held on Shankill Road and on the Falls. The Northern Ireland Government, alarmed at what looked like revolution, used all the force of the Special Powers Act and ordered the Royal Ulster Constabulary to break up the meetings. Contingents of the Royal Inniskilling Fusiliers appeared in the streets of Belfast, armed with machine-guns. The B Special Constabulary, Stormont's political police force, stood by ready for action.

There was fierce fighting between the unemployed and the state forces. The workers erected barricades. They dug up the pavements and, lacking other weapons, hurled cobblestones at the police and soldiers. Eventually, on the evening of Tuesday 11 October, the police, finding they could control the crowds no longer, opened fire. They fired indiscriminately, on Catholics and Protestants alike and they wounded five people, one of whom died a few hours later in hospital.

Next day, Wednesday 12 October, workers in the few linen mills that were still busy declared for strike action in sympathy with the unemployed. Belfast Trades Council called for a general strike. And that evening the police again opened fire, killing another man and wounding several others. Hundreds of people were arrested and thrown into prison. The veteran British trade union leader, Tom Mann, was detained by the RUC and deported from Belfast when he arrived, as representative of the National Unemployed Workers' Movement in Britain, to attend the funerals of the men who were shot dead.

On the day Tom Mann was deported the Northern Ireland Government admitted defeat. The Lord Mayor of Belfast, Sir Crawford McCullough, called local trade union leaders to a conference in the City Hall to discuss a settlement. The Board of Poor Law Guardians, cause of all the trouble, was abolished. Relief money was increased to thirty-two shillings a week.

The unity of Catholics and Protestants which forced these concessions from the government was not to last long. Soon after the Out-Door-Relief Demonstrations, Unionist leaders like Basil Brooke, J. M. Andrews, James Craig—all very wealthy men—were denouncing the Catholics as traitors and advising employers not to give them work.

At the same time a movement known as the Ulster Protestant League was propagating both Hitlerism and anti-Catholicism and attacking Labour and trade union meetings. The activities of these agitators culminated in the sectarian riots of 1935 when twelve prople were killed and hundreds of Catholic workers were again driven from their jobs and their homes.

It took the Second World War, which began in September 1939, to bring a halt, temporary though as it has turned out to be, in the almost endless sectarian war that has destroyed Labour unity in Northern Ireland.

On the trade union front, during the 1920s, the main events in the Irish Free State included the breakaway of Larkin and some of his followers from the Irish Transport and General Workers' Union and the formation of the Workers' Union of Ireland. Between 1919 and 1920 a few trade unionists, dissatisfied with the generally-evasive attitude of the British Labour movement to the question of Irish independence, broke away from the British unions of which they were members and formed Irish unions.

Before the rise of the ITGWU "the majority of Irish trade union leaders of the old school were firm believers in the value of amalgamations with British societies," though there were a few Irish unions which were jealous of their independence. Among these were the Dublin Typographical Provident Society, the Dublin Metropolitan House and Ship Painters' Union, and the Belfast Operative House Painters' Union which, in 1896, persuaded the British TUC to curb the activities of the Amalgamated Painters' Society, a British union, in Ireland.

Nonetheless, in 1907 the Irish TUC rejected a proposal, which came from the early Sinn Fein organisation, to form an Irish Federation of Trade Unions and to encourage Irish trade unionists to leave the British societies.

The Irish trade unions, as distinct from the British or cross-channel unions, gained influence and membership during the 1920s and '30s, and by the year 1936 they represented nearly half the affiliated membership of the Irish TUC. In 1939 eighteen of them, belatedly taking the advice of Sinn Fein, combined to form an Advisory Council of Irish Unions.

These unions in the ACIU resented the fact that the cross-channel unions, whose Irish membership was mainly in the Six Counties of Northern Ireland, dominated the Executive Council of the Irish TUC and determined the congress's policy.

The disagreements between British unions and Irish unions within the Irish TUC led to a split in 1944 and to the formation of the Congress of Irish Unions. The immediate cause of the split was the decision of the Executive Council of the Irish TUC to seek affiliation to the World Federation of Trade Unions. The WFTU, which Irish unions alleged was 'communist dominated' arose out of the wartime co-operation of trade unions in Britain, the USSR, the USA, France, China and other Allied countries. But underlying the split was the basic question of whether trade unions in Ireland should be Irish based and controlled or merely Irish departments of British unions.

13

AFTER THE SECOND WORLD WAR

WHEN the Second World War ended in 1945 the trade union movement in Ireland was faced with two problems. There was, first of all, the split. The movement was divided into those unions that had formed the Congress of Irish Unions and those, including many of the Irish-based unions, that had remained with the Irish TUC. When the two congresses eventually merged to form the Irish Congress of Trade Unions, in 1949, the CIU had twenty-three Irish unions, with a total membership of approximately 190,000; but there were twenty-one Irish unions in the Irish TUC and they, along with the British unions, brought the membership of the older congress to about 211,000.

Moreover, the withdrawal of the ITGWU from the Irish TUC meant that the Workers' Union of Ireland, which had hitherto been outcast as a breakaway union, was able to affiliate to the congress. Jim Larkin was still alive in 1945 and for more than twenty years he had attended the annual conferences of the Irish TUC, not as a representative of his union, the WUI, but as a delegate from the Dublin Trades Council. How the WUI came to be affiliated to the Dublin Trades Council while ineligible to be in the Irish TUC, of which the Council was part, was, apparently, a matter that nobody bothered to sort out.

The split continued for nearly ten years without much being done to bring the two congresses together, though two separate congresses with policies and views that often conflicted made industrial relations and negotiations between unions and government departments unnecessarily difficult. This was a matter about which the Government in the Republic and employers' organisations began to express concern, especially during the period of economic revival in the mid-1950s. But how was the division in the unions to be ended when the CIU insisted that all trade unions in Ireland should be 'Irish based and controlled' and that British unions should withdraw from the country.

The second problem facing the unions was the refusal of the Northern Ireland Government to have any dealings with the Irish TUC, even though as a gesture of goodwill towards Stormont the ITUC had set up a Northern Committee to deal with affairs within the Six Counties. Until the reunification of the congresses the hostility of the Stormont Government was a matter that concerned only the Irish TUC. The CIU unions had few members in Northern Ireland and were not, therefore, much implicated in relations with the Government.

Unionist politicians, including members of the Stormont Cabinet, did everything possible to exploit the rift between the ITUC and the CIU. When it became evident that the two congresses were going to merge they did everything to prevent reunification.

The Unionists had, of course, political reasons for this policy. They could hardly countenance a working-class movement that was all-Ireland based and which emphasised the economic interests of working people irrespective of partition or religion.

The argument of the Unionists was that there were 175,000 members of British unions in Northern Ireland. In addition there were 10,000 members of local, that is Northern Ireland, unions, and only 8,000 in unions that operated from the South. The British unions and the local unions should, therefore, combine and form a Northern Ireland Trades Union Congress. And such a congress, the politicians promised, would be immediately recognised by the Stormont Government.

Some trade unionists in Northern Ireland and some members of the Northern Ireland Labour Party more or less agreed with this scheme. In a paper which he read to the Statistical and Social Inquiry Society, in 1954, D. W. Bleakley, who was a Labour MP at Stormont from 1958 until 1965, and who, in 1971, was made Minister of Community Relations in the Government of Mr. Brian Faulkner, stated that:

It seems reasonable to suggest that the only solution that is likely to endure is one that recognises the essential realities of the situation . . . a federal solution may be the most suitable. Under such a scheme a TUC would be set up for the 319,000 members in the South of Ireland. This body would be controlled by, and would be responsible to the trade unionists of the Twenty-six Counties. Since only 46,000 of those belong to unions based outside Eire, it could not be argued that such a TUC was dominated by British interests. A Northern Ireland TUC could then be set up to look after the interests of trade unionists in the North. This body (like the Southern body) would be quite autonomous and would be controlled by the trade union membership in Northern Ireland. It could not be asserted that such a body was 'foreign' for there are only 8,700 trade unionists in the North belonging to unions based outside the United Kingdom.

Bleakley went on to suggest that "under such an arrangement each part of Ireland would be served by its own central trade union organisation. Matters affecting both parts of Ireland could be looked after by a joint committee of the two bodies. Later this committee might be enlarged to include representatives from the British TUC, and so trade union co-operation would be achieved on the widest possible scale."

One of the more persistent enemies of the Irish TUC at that time was Ivan Neill, Stormont's Minister of Labour. Harold Binks, who was president of the ITUC in 1956, described Neill as "one of the leading opponents of unity."

In December 1955, when the Irish TUC and the CIU began the preliminary talks that eventually brought about reunification, Neill warned "Ulster workers to beware of the dangers inherent in the proposed unification of Ulster and Eire unions." He alleged that the real motives of those who wanted trade union unity were political, part of what he described as "the struggle for the political unity of Ireland and our separation from the rest of the United Kingdom."

Among the other outspoken opponents of trade union unity were Brian Faulkner, who was Minister of Home Affairs; W. J. Fitzsimmons, who was a parliamentary secretary; R. W. B. McConnell, MP; Mr. Edmund Warnock, MP, along with the Unionist newspapers and, inevitably, the Unionist-Labour Association.

All the efforts of the Unionist politicians and of the press failed, however, to divide the unions, North and South. As W. D. Flackes wrote in the *Belfast Telegraph* on 24 July 1964:

. . . the desire for unity and solidarity among trade unionists throughout Ireland remained strong regardless of political differences . . . this fact enabled the Northern Ireland Committee to enjoy wide support even without official recognition, while proposals for a separate Ulster TUC or a Northern Ireland Committee of the British TUC have attracted little interest.

In 1954 the Irish TUC and the CIU set up a joint committee which eventually issued a *Memorandum on Trade Union Unity*. This memorandum set out the differences that divided the two congresses. The CIU insisted that "the ideal was an all-Ireland trade union movement, free from outside control, designed for the protection and security of Irish workers," and suggested that "if adequate guarantees and proper guidance were given to the Irish members of British unions a substantial number of such members would consent to form or join Irish unions, thereby enabling the Congresses to proceed with the establishment of an all-Ireland trade union centre which would be Irish-based and controlled in all its parts."

Against this view, the Irish TUC pointed out that while the majority of members of the British unions did not want to create a separate Northern Ireland TUC, and so split the movement politically, they would nonetheless not consent to leaving the British unions. The Irish TUC stated that "an all-Ireland trade union centre which would be Irish based and controlled in all its parts was not possible."

Despite these differences the two congresses agreed to the formation of a Provisional United Trade Union Organisation which, under the chairmanship of Professor John Busteed of University College, Cork, patiently examined all the arguments on both sides and eventually produced a proposed constitution for a united congress of the trade unions.

The unions spent two years discussing and amending and deciding whether to accept or reject the constitution. Finally, in 1959, the Irish TUC and the Congress of Irish Unions merged to form one body, the Irish Congress of Trade Unions which united the trade unions, North and South, British and Irish.

The ICTU took over the organisation of the Irish TUC, including the Committee in Northern Ireland. The Northern Committee soon found that following the merger the Stormont Government had become even more antagonistic. It took another five years, a lot of back-room pressure and argument, and a change of government at Stormont before the Unionist politicians made peace with the trade unions and recognised the ICTU's Northern Committee.

In 1962, when Lord Brookeborough was still Premier at Stormont, the unions were told that if they wanted the Government to have any dealings with the Northern Committee "their first step would be to disassociate themselves from the ICTU."

Brookeborough said the Government could not recognise the ICTU because it was controlled from Dublin, and that the Northern Committee, with which he was being asked to deal, had no autonomy within Northern Ireland. Unfortunately, the constitution of the ICTU presented him with another argument for ignoring the committee. Until it was amended in 1970, the constitution provided that a majority of places on the ICTU's Executive Council would be reserved for the Irish-based unions.

The conflict between the ICTU and the Stormont Government was causing difficulties which the employers, apart altogether from the unions, seemed to be concerned about. It was impossible, for instance, to form a Northern Ireland productivity council. The Government would not accept the representative whom the ICTU insisted upon nominating. For the same reason the setting up of a Northern Ireland economic council was delayed for a long time. The appointment of union representatives to arbitration councils, national insurance tribunals and similar bodies was also unduly delayed, sometimes for years.

In 1963 the National Association of British Manufacturers, through its Northern Ireland Committee, stated in a pamphlet that "the non-recognition of the Irish Congress of Trade Unions represents an absolute bar to co-operation in Northern Ireland."

The question of recognition was then taken up by the Churches Industrial Council, an inter-denominational body that had been set up in October 1959 to combat what was believed to be the decline of moral standards and the spread of communist influence in industry. Clergymen from the main churches, including the Catholic Church, industrial employers, trade unionists and prominent individuals were associated with the Council.

When the CIC approached the Stormont Government about recognition of the ICTU they found that the main opponents of the congress were the Unionist back-benchers. One back-bencher told the CIC that the ICTU was a threat to the sovereignty of Northern Ireland and that any government which recognised the congress would not survive.

The CIC also found that some Unionist back-benchers were hostile not only to the Irish TUC but "to trade unions in general." Members of the council had to make it clear to these gentlemen that in modern industrial democracies trade unions are part of the social framework and that governments and employers usually try to work with the unions in efforts to overcome problems in industry.

Other organisations besides the CIC were seeking to change the Stormont Government's attitude. The Northern Ireland Committee of the NABM asked J. L. Montrose, an academic lawyer at Queen's University, to advise on the most suitable wording that would so alter the rules of the ICTU as to give the Northern Committee autonomy and at the same time overcome the objections of the Unionist back-benchers.

Finally, in the summer of 1964, the Stormont Government accepted the case put to them by the CIC and the NABM, and the ICTU altered its rules so as to give the Northern Committee autonomy to deal with affairs within Northern Ireland. By this compromise the organisational unity of the Irish Congress of Trade Unions was maintained and the way prepared for co-operation by the Stormont Government, the Northern Committee of the ICTU and employers' organisations.

The honeymoon has now grown into a happy marriage and today, 1972, co-operation between the Stormont Government and the Northern Committee of the ICTU has reached the point where the Government is paying the committee a grant of £10,000 a year. Under an arrangement with the Irish National Productivity Council the Government in Dublin has, for many years, been paying a similar grant to the ICTU organisation in the Republic.

But this certainly does not mean that every trade unionist in Ireland is now happy and satisfied. Recognition by the Stormont Government of the ICTU has not in the least improved the economic situation in the Six Counties. It has certainly not lowered the abnormally high unemployment in that part of Ireland. And it has not altered the outlook of those union members who, in the words of a report later compiled by the CIC, "saw reconciliation as a threat to their strength in terms of militancy."

The trade unions will always have militant members. History indeed proves that there would never have been any trade union movement without them.

The trade unions of modern Ireland have come a long way from the days when their members were imprisoned, fined, whipped through the streets of Dublin, deported, or forced to emigrate. Today there are some ninety unions affiliated to the Irish Congress of Trade Unions, with a total membership of more than 560,000 all over Ireland. These unions represent all sorts of employees, from local council labourers and skilled tradesmen to actors, civil servants and airline pilots. And as time goes on trade unionism spreads more and more to the professional middle classes, to technicians, managers and administrators. Among the unions which have come to the fore in Ireland during the past twenty-five years are unions like the National Union of Journalists which now has about 1,300 members in this country, or like the Association of Scientific, Technical, and Managerial Staffs which is one of the fastest-growing unions in Ireland or in Britain. The AST&MS has about 8,000 members in Ireland.

The development of social services in what is called the welfare state, economic planning by governments in Ireland as well as elsewhere, more sophisticated methods of settling disputes in industry, labour courts, tribunals, committees of inquiry etc.— all mean that the trade unions have today greater responsibilities than at any time in their history.

But with all these changes, and even though the unions appoint representatives to serve on all kinds of boards and councils and are interested in everything from child welfare to the promotion of tourism, the essential purpose of trade union- ism, which is securing adequate wages and proper working con- ditions for the members, remains today what it was in the early eighteenth century, when the Irish trade unions first attracted the attention of parliament.

14

CHALLENGE OF THE GRIM FUTURE

IF THE essential purpose of trade unions is to secure adequate wages for their members and to safeguard terms and conditions of employment then the main problems which unions will face, in Ireland and elsewhere during the 1980s, will be unemployment, the effects of inflation, and attempts by the state to impose legal restraints on strikes, on wages bargaining, and even on trade union membership.

Inflation puts trade unions everywhere in a position where they find it impossible to improve real wages, i.e. the living standards of their members. As soon as a wages increase is obtained its value is eroded by rising prices. Consequently even to maintain the pre- vailing value of wages, increases must always be at least equal to the rate of inflation. Collective bargaining becomes defensive.

This form of collective bargaining has resulted in wages claims being advanced year by year, and annual wages increases corres- pondingly anticipated. As soon as one claim is settled negotia- tions for a new increase begin. In the Republic of Ireland these annual wages claims are called National Pay Rounds.

In the 20 years between 1946 and 1966 there were ten National Pay Rounds, an average of one every two years. In the ten years between 1968 and 1978 there were a further nine National Pay Rounds, an average of one every thirteen months. Since 1974 negotiating the National Pay Round has become an annual responsibility for unions and employers in the Republic.

In Britain and in Northern Ireland wages increases are not classified as National Rounds, but nearly all British and Northern

Ireland unions now make separate annual claims for increases. And if government policy continues to be that of the present Conservative administration in Britain wages bargaining will become increasingly difficult for the policy of Government in 1984 (at least) was to keep wages increases below the current rate of inflation, thus in effect lowering the living standards of employees.

Continually rising unemployment is the next serious problem. In an interview with *The Sunday Press* (June 1980) Senator Fintan Kennedy, retiring President of the Irish Transport and General Workers' Union, expressed the view that unemployment would be one of the worst problems which not only the unions but also all the rest of society would have to deal with. In his opinion, unemployment — and he was referring primarily to the Republic of Ireland — "might come dangerously close to causing an explosion of discontent, especially among young people who cannot find jobs".

The same fear is held by political and industrial leaders everywhere — in Britain, where unemployment reached more than 3,000,000 after five years of Conservative Government, and in Europe, where predictions put the total number of people who will be out of work in 1985 at 35,000,000. Unemployment in Ireland in December 1984 was 225,445 in the Republic of Ireland, and 119,401 in Northern Ireland.

Unemployment not only diminishes the bargaining power of the trade unions, it also reduces their membership. During what is sometimes called "the current economic recession" unemployment has been heaviest in the manufacturing industries, the very industries where there have always been high levels of union membership. How this affects union membership was explained at the 1982 annual conference of the Irish Congress of Trade Unions where delegates were told the total membership of affiliated unions had decreased by 13 per cent.

In Northern Ireland the trade unions have been complaining about high unemployment for more than 30 years, but their complaints seem to have been unheeded. Neither the Stormont Government, which was the government of Northern Ireland until 1972, nor the Secretaries of State for Northern Ireland appointed since then have been able to reduce unemployment or to ensure what was once a national aim, viz. a high and stable level of employment. Perhaps this is not possible, for in the context of the United Kingdom economy Northern Ireland is the worst of what used to be called "the distressed areas".

The economic development of Northern Ireland is restricted by the absence of basic heavy industry such as steel-smelting, the absence of indigenous minerals in workable deposits, a comparatively small and relatively improverished consumer market, political and economic isolation from the Republic of Ireland, isolation from the rest of the United Kingdom by the expense of sea and air transport, and isolation by distance from Western Europe.

These are serious economic and geographical disadvantages. In addition Northern Ireland's political instability and propensity to engage in communal violence also discourage industrial growth because they discourage investment.

Northern Ireland Government policy since as early as 1945 was designed to attract firms from Britain, from the United States and from other foreign countries. For a period in the 1950s and early 1960s this policy was modestly successful, though it meant the paying of very generous subsidies, grants and other inducements to those firms which agreed to set up branches of their business in Northern Ireland. It also involved the risk that these migrant firms would accept the subsidies, provide employment for a longer or shorter period, and then close down, either because of economic recession or because more profitable sites were being offered by governments elsewhere.

Among the major firms which have settled in and have later left Northern Ireland have been Courtaulds, I.C.I. and British Enkalon. Today the authorities admit that because of violence and economic recession it is almost impossible to get firms to come into Northern Ireland. The attraction of new firms is therefore no longer a way of reducing unemployment.

The difficulties of Northern Ireland have been recognised and acknowledged by an official government committee of inquiry which stated in 1976 that:

... as far as employment goes the long term prospects are distinctly unattractive. Northern Ireland as a regional economy possessing a strong mixed industrial structure, competitive on the basis of high productivity and capable of generating more of its own growth is not a realisable goal.

Despite these inescapably unpleasant facts and the government's own gloomy forecast the Irish Congress of Trade Unions in Northern Ireland remains optimistic and has participated, along with government and employers' organisations, in state-appointed economic councils and industrial development associations. Since 1956 there have been four Northern Ireland Economic Councils. The most recently created development association is the Industrial Development Board. The trade unions are represented on both.

It would seem, by the way, that the difference between economic councils and development boards is that the former are merely advisory whereas the latter are expected to show results.

The 1982 annual conference of the Irish Congress of Trade Unions proposed that the Government embark immediately on an economic plan which, the ICTU claimed, would create 40,000 jobs in one year at an investment cost of £750 million. Whether such a plan would have government support, or would be successful is always doubtful. Indeed experience has shown that attempts to plan the economic development of Northern Ireland, even when backed and financed by government, have failed. There was such a plan in 1965, and another in 1970. They both failed and had to be abandoned.

The political entity known officially as Northern Ireland was created by the 1920 Government of Ireland Act which partitioned Ireland, leaving the six north-eastern counties under an Ulster Unionist Government. That this so-called "experiment in devolution" has been a failure, economically, politically and constitutionally has been admitted even by British Cabinet Ministers and senior civil servants, but it would be virtually impossible to get many trade union members in Northern Ireland to admit likewise. If Northern trade union officials, or delegates to ICTU conferences, were also to say that Northern Ireland was a failure they would be denounced immediately as enemies of the state and alienated, even more than they are at present, from the majority of trade union members. Yet the partition of Ireland, apart from its many other undesirable consequences, has been a most serious obstacle in the way of trade union progress and development.

Because of partition the Irish Congress of Trade Unions is only nominally an all-Ireland movement; it is little more than a "bridge" between trade unions in Northern Ireland and trade unions in the Republic of Ireland. This has become increasingly evident within the past ten or twelve years. The reason is that the social, economic, political and legal problems that trade unions in Northern Ireland have to deal with differ in innumerable ways from the problems of the southern unions. Most trade unions in Northern Ireland are integrated with the British unions. The unions in the Republic of Ireland are less so. Moreover, the British Parliament and Government adopt a somewhat more aggressive attitude to trade unions than Dail Eireann or the Government of the Republic of Ireland.

These are weaknesses in the structure of the ICTU which those who still campaign for a breakaway Six County TUC are always ready to exploit. Indeed there have been recent and quite serious plots to detach the unions in Northern Ireland from the ICTU, and one or two trade union officials in Northern Ireland have been reprimanded by their headquarters in Britain for lending support to those who promoted these plots.

An even more serious threat to the ICTU within the past twelve years has been the emergence among industrial workers of organisations such as the Loyalist Association of Workers (LAW) and later the Ulster Workers' Council (UWC). The names of these organisations signify their political motivation and their association not only with Orangeism and Paisleyism but also with more dangerous movements like the Ulster Defence Association (UDA) and the Ulster Volunteer Force (UVF).

The LAW originated in the Belfast shipbuilding industry about 1970, its main objective being to secure the immediate internment of "all known Republicians". The UWC, which eventually replaced LAW, was responsible for the political general strike which in May 1974 forced the resignation of the inter-party, power-sharing Northern Ireland Executive and the abandonment of the proposed Council of Ireland. The power-sharing executive and the Council of Ireland had been agreed in the autumn of 1973 at a conference of British Cabinet Ministers, representatives of the Government of the Irish Republic, and leaders of the main political parties in Northern Ireland. It was subsequently approved by the British Parliament, and approved by an elected assembly in Northern Ireland.

The UWC strike was, therefore, a challenge to democracy and the rule of law as it operates in these islands. Yet the British Government, then led by the Labour Prime Minister Harold Wilson, capitulated to the strikers. British Army contingents in Ulster stayed safely in their barracks. The Royal Ulster Constabulary stood by while the UWC, the UDA and other people from the Protestant paramilitary organisations blocked the highways, prevented the normal working of industry, and threatened peaceful citizens. The UWC strike succeeded because the state allowed itself to be intimidated by working-class fascism.

The Irish Congress of Trade Unions was helpless in that strike. But with the encouragement of the British Government and assisted personally by Len Murray, General Secretary of the Trades Union Congress, ICTU organised what was intended to be a march of the strikers back to work on 20 May. It was a futile gesture. Only a few workmen dared defy the Loyalist pickets. Brian Faulkner, Chief Executive in the power-sharing administration under threat from the Loyalists, later recorded:

Only about two hundred people, most of them trade union officials, turned up for the 'Back to Work' march and though they completed their gesture by walking into the shipyard in the face of jeers and a barrage of rotten vegetables hurled by 'pickets' it was a futile display of courage.

The threat of paramilitary power hangs permanently over the trade union movement in Northern Ireland. When, for example, the movement known as the Peace People in 1976 organised a mass demonstration on Shankill Road — Belfast's main Protestant ghetto — the UDA let it be known that under no circumstances would the ICTU be allowed to join the march. And at the annual conference of ICTU in 1982 Thomas Smyth, an official of the Union of Construction Workers', Allied Trades and Technicians, warned that nearly all the construction work being done in the city of Belfast was in the control of other paramilitary terrorists who decided what workmen should and should not be employed. These terrorists, said Mr Smyth, set themselves up as "sub-contractors" on the building sites and then compelled the legitimate contractors to pay them protection money. And on some sites this protection money could amount to as much as £500 a week.

Trade unions by themselves are powerless to deal with such criminals, who, having behind them the power of the gun and the midnight knock on a man's front door, can defy the police and can threaten with death anyone who defies them. One very serious threat is that these criminals may try to infiltrate the trade unions and control them from within.

Meanwhile the trade unions in the Republic of Ireland have been comparatively safe from the threats and pressures to which the Northern unions are subjected, but they too have been criticised, especially by academics whose profession is to study industrial relations, employment laws, trade union attitudes and forms of organisation.

One criticism is that trade unions in the Republic of Ireland are noted for their tenacity when on strike, and also for their propensity to "poach" members from one another and to engage in inter-union disputes. These inter-union disputes are now controlled by an ICTU rule which requires that at least 80 per cent of the workers "in a grade, group, category or establishment" must signify their desire to transfer from one union to another. If less than this proportion want to change unions nobody is allowed to change.

Trade unions in the Republic of Ireland are still organisationally influenced by developments in the nineteenth century when British unions and unions in Southern Ireland were more closely linked than they are today. In the Thomas Davis Lectures entitled *Trade Unions and Change in Irish Society,* Professor Michael P Fogarty from the Public Studies Institute in London thought it "somewhat ironic that Irish trade unions have imitated the English model of organisation ... and that after sixty years of independence the Irish pattern of trade union organisation is still essentially English". Professor Fogarty was presumably referring to unions in the Republic of Ireland, not to the unions in Northern Ireland. Trade unionists in Northern Ireland are unlikely to see anything "ironic" in the fact that their unions are still essentially British. That is what they would want.

Trade unions in Britain have been so moulded by their own history that today there are craft unions, industrial unions, general unions, service unions, and unions of professional and technical employees all affiliated to the British Trades Union Congress. Trade union membership now covers the whole range of employment from the unskilled labourers of the general unions to some of the more highly paid technicians, managers, and even directors. Affiliations to the ICTU follow much the same pattern.

Critics of this seemingly haphazard structure, which results often in several unions operating in one firm and is frequently the cause of the inter-union rivalry so often deplored in the Republic, believe that the trade unions should be reshaped into industrial blocs, like the industrial unions of the USSR, Sweden and the Federal German Republic. Those who deplore the historical influence of British trade unionism in Ireland would like to see the Irish trade unions reshaped into these industrial blocs — one union for each separate industry. This is called the "rationalisation" of trade union organisation.

Trade unions in Britain and in both parts of Ireland have resisted most schemes for rationalisation. The British TUC and the ICTU both take the view that amalgamations and mergers of unions should be voluntary, and with the consent of the members, not undertaken merely to satisfy some master plan, usually devised by academics remote from industry, for the creation of fewer and more uniformly organised unions.

In any case, reorganising the trade unions into industrial blocs is far from being among the present-day priorities of the Irish trade union movement. The struggle for survival during the 1980s and beyond will be determined by those three dire threats — unemployment, inflation, and restrictive legislation.

KERR'S EXPOSITION

OF

LEGISLATIVE TYRANNY,

AND

DEFENCE

OF

THE TRADES' UNION.

Oppression may its hostile front display,
And tyranny exist its short accursed day,
But unashamed virtue and the cause of right
Shall stand undaunted, nor will yield to might

KERR.

RESPECTFULLY DEDICATED
TO THE
TRADES' UNIONISTS OF GREAT BRITAIN & IRELAND

BELFAST:

PRINTED BY J. SMYTH, 34, HIGH-STREET.

1834.

The original cover of a pamphlet written by George Kerr, a Belfast trade unionist, in 1834 describing how he was arrested and imprisoned when he went to Derry to form a union for the local cabinetmakers. Reprinted in full, the pamphlet is a valuable source material for a history of the trade unions in Ireland.

APPENDIX I

NOTHING has of late engrossed more of the public attention, nor occupied more space of the magazines and journals of the present day, than the subject of Trades Unions. Hitherto, it was hard to find any journal or magazine deigning to take the least notice of the working class of society, unless for the purpose of stigmatizing them with the cognomens of *mob, lower order, swinish multitude,* or the *rabble.*

These terms, with which they were so often assailed, serve to show the working classes of the present day, that they had been in former times much degraded in society, either by their own misconduct, or by the despotic sway of their more opulent neighbours. And although times have altered greatly, within the few last years, still are they often saluted by the old epithets by those who, while they cannot but acknowledge that the mighty influence of the schoolmaster has been the means of effecting a great improvement in their intellectual condition, yet at the same time perceive that the only way to aggrandize themselves is by keeping the working classes continually in an abject state of slavery and thraldom, that they might be able to rise to wealth and affluence on their ruins.

It is, however, matter of consolation, to think that the working classes are now able to produce both journals and weekly periodicals of their own, and though they are as yet few in number, there is little doubt but they will become, ere long, more numerous, and consequently, more extensively circulated. In fact, I know of no better plan for concentrating the intelligence of the working classes, and promoting their best interests, than by employing the public press in their own behalf; for it unfortunately happens, that out of all the periodicals of the present day, who, as I have formerly remarked, are honouring the working classes with so much of their attention, there are fifty opposed to the interests of the Trades Unions, for one that espouses their cause. And it is also no less true, that the upper ranks of society hardly ever, if at all, read those publications that are favourable to the rights of industry; and indeed were one to talk to some of these gentry on the rights of industry, they would, I dare say, tell you, that the phrase having never occurred to them, they should take the trouble of consulting their vocabulary, to ascertain whether any such term was to be found. At all events, no one can deny, that in all movements of the working classes, the general cry has been—"Down with the rebels! they are about to endanger the peace of society, and annihilate the social compact by which the community are knit together, by destroying the free commerce of the country." Such I know to be the case, and who has not seen it too frequently exemplified? It matters little what are the objects they have in view; it matters little how well or faithfully they are able to vindicate the integrity of their motives, or the justice of their cause:—the truth is, they have long been accustomed to the iron yoke. "And why" say their oppressors, "should they be discontented now?" "We," they say, "have always been their governors, by hereditary descent; and although we cannot claim the privilege of having more judgement than they; still do we claim the privilege of having more wealth in our possessions; nor are we so foolishly blind as not to know that wealth is the standard by which humanity is valued, and that knowledge, which is said to be power, is but a bagatelle compared to wealth;" therefore, say they, "let us act on the universal axiom; let them take who have the power, and let them keep who can."

These foregoing remarks are, I think, a fair and candid statement of the relative position in which the working classes stand to the more wealthy portion of the community; and if any thing were wanting to prove it, we have the woful examples before us, of the harsh and inhuman treatment of the Trades Unionists that are every where taking place. And as I myself happen to be among the persecuted number, and as I have been requested by several of my friends to expose the treatment I received, I shall here detail the circumstances exactly as they occurred.

About the month of January last, having occasion to be in Londonderry; while in that city, I made it my business to have a meeting with some of the Cabinet-makers, in order to learn the state of their trade; and also to acquaint them of the state of the Cabinet-makers' trade in Belfast, to which last mentioned body I belonged. After mutual explanation on both sides, it was at length agreed, that as there had been a great falling off, and frequent reduction of the Cabinet-maker's wages, to the extent of thirty, forty, and in some instances even sixty per cent, we came to the determination of joining the Trades' Union, or Friendly Society, which had for its object the unity of all Cabinet-makers in the three kingdoms; that they might the more effectually be enabled to support their sick, and bury their dead; and that they might be enabled to support their idle brothers who could not get employment, and also to support the travelling operative, who wandered from town to town in quest of employment, and in short to endeavour by every means in our power to check the evils of society, by recommending and providing to our members the means of moral and intellectual improvement.

This being accomplished, I left the city of Londonderry with two other friends who accompanied me, and arrived again in Belfast, congratulating our friends on our return on the happy and felicitous prospects which were likely to occur from such a laudable and honourable Union. Yet, notwithstanding the consistency of our principles, and the equity of our designs, the evil eye of suspicion rested on our workings, and conceiving that the Union which we had raised up for a good and for a noble purpose, was fraught with mischief, the Mayor of Londonderry raised the arm of persecution against us, and arrested two of the Cabinet-makers of Londonderry, and after using threats and menaces to induce them to give evidence that the two other individuals and myself who visited Londonderry, administered unlawful oaths to them and others, he incarcerated them in the gaol, and swore by his immortal God, that he would transport them if they did not swear to the foregoing effect; they were, however, admitted to bail, to appear and prosecute at the assizes on March last, in Londonderry; and a warrant was also issued for the apprehension of the two individuals and myself, who went to Londonderry as before-mentioned; the warrant was sent to Belfast, and one of my colleagues was arrested, and sent on to the Mayor of Londonderry, who interrogated him, and threatened him in like manner as he had done to others. He was then sent to the gaol, and the Assizes being commenced, he was brought forward for trial, but upon the non-appearance of prosecutors, he was admitted to bail, himself in £100, and two sureties in £10 each, to appear when called on. There were also a great many Sawyers (who had also been apprehended) brought up for trial at the same time, on a similar charge:—the Mayor having caused the house in which they were assembled, to be surrounded by the police, &c. and although they were sitting peaceably together, discoursing on the affairs connected with their labour, they also were to be tried as conspirators against the laws of their country, and as being an unlawful combination held together by secret ties of the most revolting kind. It is needless to say that they also were bailed out to appear if again called on; and one of the two individuals whom he first arrested (for the purpose of making him prosecute the two other individuals and myself,) was indicted to stand his trial for perjury; because, through the threats of the Mayor, he was so much staggered, as to be in a great measure, incapable of knowing what he said, and thereby happened to contradict his statements. And the other person who was bound over to prosecute, did not appear.

Shortly after the Assizes, however, this same person who failed to appear as prosecutor, was again arrested and sent to jail, where he was kept for a week or two, and was then admitted to bail, and as far as I am given to understand, is the person who is bound to prosecute me, as I was immediately thereafter arrested in Belfast court-house, whither I had gone to hear a trial which was to take place. As soon as I was arrested, I was sent to the House of Correction, where I remained for the space of about two hours, and was then sent off, like some thief or murderer, guarded by four police-men, with loaded muskets, two of them leaving me as soon as they had escorted me a short distance from the town. I arrived in Antrim same evening, and was locked up in the bridewell for the night; and the following morning, Sunday, a friend who had come after me, hired another car to take me onwards, as the one which took me from Belfast to Antrim, had returned on the Saturday night.

We set out from Antrim after breakfast-time, with another couple of police from the Antrim station, and went on in the like manner from station to station, with the exception of walking part of the road; I being of course given up to the police charge at each station, who always sent a couple of their men on with me, and each couple of course returned back to their own quarters, after leaving me at the station beyond theirs. I slept at Garvagh next night, Sabbath, and reached Londonderry on the evening of Monday, where I was again delivered up to the police, who took me to the Mayor's house, who soon appeared, and asked, "who I was that they had in custody?" And on learning the same, he asked me "if I was chairman at the later Belfast meeting, which was held for the purpose of petitioning for the clemency of the Crown in behalf of the six Dorchester Unionists?" To which question I answered in the affirmative. He then asked me several questions, and amongst the rest, he asked me, "if I was a Trades Unionist?" To which I replied, I was happy to inform him I was; and immediately asked him for what reason he had caused me to be dragged so far from my home, in such an ignominious manner? But the only answer he deigned to give me, was this—"The Attorney General will inform you,"—At once as laconic as he was sarcastic. I then offered to produce bail for my appearance at the Assizes. He asked me then who were the persons I meant to produce as bailsmen?" and as they were present I pointed them out, at the same time naming them.

He immediately objected to the one, as being (as he said) a Trades Union man. I asked was he certain that a Trades Union man was a bad man? He then said it mattered nothing whether he was or not; he would not take a Trades Union man as bail. I said this was treating me rather harshly; as, in the first place, it did not matter whether the bailsmen were Trades Unionists or not, provided they were able to pay the forfeit, on my non-appearance; and on the other hand, I said it was pre-judging the question before the trial; but he still insisted that he would take no Union-man as bail. To which I again remonstrated, saying, that on account of my being a stranger in Londonderry, it would perhaps be difficult for me to procure men to bail me, who were not either Trades' Union-men, Ribbon-men, or perhaps Orangemen. *This last I said, having heard that he himself was an Orangeman.* However, it was all to no purpose; as he then ordered me to be taken to his office, where he would immediately follow and settle the matter there.

We were not long in the office before the Mayor, who appeared with the Clerk of the Peace, and during the interim my friend had gone in quest of other bailsmen. The Mayor asked what amount of bail the former prisoner gave? I told him he gave two sureties in £10 each, and himself in £100; but as he did not recollect exactly the amount himself, he sent a person out of the office to make enquiry, who satisfied him as to the truth of the former statement. The person whom he had sent to enquire stated, at the same time, that Baron Pennefather, who was judge of the Assizes, deemed it best to take the small amount of bail specified, in consequence of the prisoner being a stranger in Londonderry, and consequently might have some difficulty in procuring a higher amount of bail; but the Mayor of Londonderry did not seem disposed to be so courteous as the honourable Baron; for when I produced two or three other individuals, who were both able and willing to bail me to the amount taken for the other prisoner, the Mayor with the tact and ingenuity of a legislative connoisseur remarked, that the case differed between the other prisoner and me, inasmuch as he was there at the assizes and ready to take his trial. I said the case was in no way different, as the other prisoner went to Londonderry, only, when he was arrested, and I certainly did the same, and that I was ready to take my trial at any period, and that so far from my shrinking from investigation I rather courted it, as the late Belfast meeting of which I was chairman petitioned, in addition to the avowed object of their meeting, viz. (the pardon of the six unfortunate Dorchester convicts) that the House of Commons do investigate by a special committee, the nature and objects of the Trades Unions. However, it would not do; every thing was useless as he seemed determined to punish me, by committing me, at least for a time, into the gaol; for when the individuals came forward to bail me, he would not accept of them, unless they would swear that they were worth double the amount of bail, free of all debts, dues and demands; this he knew would have the desired effect, as from his knowledge of the individuals, he was assured they were not able conscientiously to do so. I again remonstrated against such inhumane treatment, and repeated, that I courted investigation as much as he, and said, so conscious was I of the purity of our principles, and the rectitude of our designs; that if the promotion of virtue and morality could be constituted a crime, then—and then only, was I guilty of one, and the Trades' Union also, with which I was connected, and that I did not care by what tribunal I was tried, even although his Britannic Majesty presided over it; but no sooner had I said this, than the Mayor threatened to commit me to prison for contempt of court, and he was followed up in his observation by the clerk. I then replied by saying that as I had never been arraigned before any court in my life time, if I had said anything wrong, it arose from my ignorance of court proceedings, as I was not aware what reverence was due to a person placed in his official situation, and if I had been guilty of a breach of order, I could only beg pardon for so doing. The Mayor replied, that as to himself he did not care; but he would not sit on that seat and hear his Majesty's name spoken disrespectfully of. To this last remark I replied, that I was unconscious of having spoken disrespectfully of His Majesty's name; and my feelings respecting him were such, that I would not sanction any disrespectful language towards him in others, much less would I be guilty of any thing of the kind myself. However, the Mayor soon cut the dialogue short, by telling me, that I must give in twenty-four hours notice of bail, as he would take bail in no other way, and immediately I was sent to the gaol, where I was kept from the evening of Monday until the forenoon of Wednesday, when I was again taken to the Mayor's office, being provided with bail to the amount last stated; but when they came forward, another obstacle arose; he said he had been considering the matter, and he found that he would have to double the amount of bail, on hearing which one of my friends went and employed an attorney to settle the matter, who came into the court and requested the Mayor to be guided by the amount of bail which Baron Pennefather had stipulated, and allowed as sufficient for the former prisoner. But the Mayor still insisted that the case was completely different betwixt he and I, *although we were both apprehended on the same charge;* and he said he would not take less than twice the amount of bail for me, which bail was also produced; but then he was determined it should not be taken, as he adopted his former plan of making them qualify for twice the amount of bail which they gave in.

My attorney again remonstrated, upon which the Mayor said—he had no wish to throw any difficulty in the way of my getting bail. My attorney replied that he was afriad, that if he persisted in his determination of making the bailsmen swear that they were worth double the amount of the sum for which they were to give bail, it would have that effect; but he would not be diverted from his purpose. We then offered to give four persons who would qualify for £20 each, and give bail for £10 each, but this also was refused, and the sheriff who was present, as if afraid that the bail proffered would be accepted, immediately said that he himself would not accept of such bail, and on being asked his reason, he said, that in the event of the prisoner's non-appearance, they would have to look for the forfeited bail from four individuals instead of two. And indeed the sheriff's remark showed so well what was passing in his mind, and the transcendant abilities of the individual who was gifted with such powers of utterance, that I could not help thinking within myself, that Solomon in all his glory and with all his wisdom spoke nothing like thee; but then again, one of Solomon's proverbs came to my recollection, which says, "A fool is known by the multitude of his words;" and another way of thinking immediately took possession of my mind, and I was grieved to think that the minds of men are so apt to be led to incorrect conclusions. But, (pardon my digression) I have already said that the Mayor would not take the proffered bail. My attorney made some further remarks on the case, and certainly evinced an eager desire to serve me, as he urged all he could the injustice done me, by the treatment I was receiving, and stated that it was punishing me previous to my having been proved guilty of a crime, and as soon as he had concluded, I again began to talk of the injustice, of prejudging the matter; but had not proceeded far, when the late Mayor, whose name is Desert, or Dysart, very humanely ejaculated, "hold your tongue sir," which certainly to say the least of it, was a little on the north side of friendly; nevertheless, stunned as I was by such unwonted conduct towards me, I had to remember that I was in the hands of ————————, and I had again recourse to the proverbs of Solomon. The first that struck me was this, "In the multitude of counsellors there is wisdom." But, as I could not persuade myself to believe that all I had heard, either from the two Mayors, or the sheriff, approached to any thing like extraordinary wisdom, I had recourse to a homely proverb before I could find any ease in my mind, it is this, "Put a beggar on horseback and he will ride." This proverb could only be gratifying to a mind like mine, as I was in a curious state at the time; and I think some one whispered in my ear, while I was in the court, that the late Mayor (who ordered me to hold my tongue) had sprung up from very poor circumstances to the situation of Mayor of Londonderry, if so, the more credit he has by it; *that is to say if he gained it honourably*. But to the point. The Mayor declared he would take no bail, but two sureties in £20 each, and myself in £100, adding with an air of malicious exultation, that it was a strange thing, that in all this mighty Union two individuals could not be found, who would qualify for £40. My attorney then gave notice that the bail should be settled by four o'clock same afternoon; and we had already one person who would give the bail asked, and were about getting another, when the Mayor, who had left the court, was met by my attorney, to whom he said, he would take no bail at all, until he should consult the Crown Counsel on the subject, which of course put a stop to further exertions at that time for bail; and at four o'clock the Mayor entered the office again, and repeated what he had formerly said to the Attorney, that he would not take bail at all without consulting the Crown.

So that here was prevarication after prevarication; and whatever honour belongs to the official situation, or to the name of Mayor of Londonderry, I think I have sufficiently proved that there is little in the man, and I regret to say it. But such conduct I shall ever hold up to detestation; for although golden linked chains may adorn his neck, the brightest and the purest chain in my estimation, is the plain unvarnished chain of truth, linked in the ties of humanity. Not being allowed to bail, I was of course sent back to my old quarters, the gaol, and on the morning of Friday was taken into a place where they keep the prison clothes, and while a suit was being looked out for me, I was ordered to give up every thing in my possession, which were all noted down. I was then ordered to strip off my clothes, which I did all to my shirt, but was ordered to take that off also, which I had to do, and also was compelled to stand naked before three of the keepers, and hold my hands above my head and cough, previous to my receiving any of the prison apparel. Thus heaping infamy and degradation upon one, who ever did and ever will despise to do any thing to my neighbour, however humble he might be, were he placed in my power. I was next taken to another part of the prison, and there secured in a ward, No. 2, over which was painted, "Committed to the assizes,"—which led me to think that I should not be released until that time. I had not been long in this ward, until the barber made his appearance, and commenced to shave me, taking directions from one of the turn-keys who was present, as to the style in which he was to operate; and not content with giving me one of the roughest scrapes he possibly could, *as it was so severe, I thought he meant to take skin and all with him.* He also at the command of the turnkey, made a very indiscriminate attack upon my whiskers, scraping the one half of them entirely off, and pruning the other, and finished his operations by making free with the hair of my head.

In the forenoon of the same day, the Governor asked me if ever I broke any stones, as I would have to do so while in the prison. I solicited him not to compel me to do this, as I would be more honourably employed at working in a tradesman-like capacity. I was then allowed to work along with three others in the carpenter's shop, where I assisted them in their work until the afternoon of Monday, when the Mayor had consented to take bail for me, viz: two sureties in £20 each, and myself in £100; thus being exactly eight days in the gaol of Londonderry. But it may here be necessary to enumerate a few more of the blessings of a gaol confinement. In the mornings, the bell rings at half-past five, when the prisoners have to get out of their hammock, which is suspended by two ring bolts from each end of the cell, one person only allowed to each cell. There is neither bed nor pillow in the hammock, but two pair of double blankets, in which one must roll themselves up in the best way they can; and as soon as the bell rings, the prisoners must get up and put their clothes on, and also fold up their blankets in a certain form, and have their cells cleaned out before six o'clock, when a second bell rings, and the turnkeys and governor come round and open the prisoners' cells; and should any of their cells be dirty, or their blankets not properly folded, they are subjected to a fine, that is, their breakfast milk, or their supper, or some portion of their victuals is kept from them; and when the fault is of greater consequence, they are put in solitary confinement for a time, not exceeding three days. As soon as the cells are open, the prisoners are marched down stairs in military like form, each bearing his chamber vase in his hand, with the night's contents; and as soon as they arrive at the lower part of the ward, a halt is made, when they are ordered to number off. When he that has been longest in the ward commences, all the rest standing in a straight line, and repeat one, two, three, &c. when the turnkey immediately says,—"To the right about—go;" and the prisoners then go outside and empty their vases, then clean themselves and prepare for work by half-past six, when they are let out of the ward, and joining the others, form a line and number off as before; and on receiving the command —"To the right about—go," away they march to their respective places of work. At nine o'clock, morning, the bell again rings for breakfast, and the same ceremony of numbering off goes on, before they are marched off to breakfast, which they get in their separate wards. The breakfast consists of a quart of porridge, or (as they call it) stir-about, with a pint of sweet milk. Work again commences at ten, when they are summoned in the usual way to it. The dinner bell rings at two o'clock, when they receive each a certain quantity of potatoes, with a pint of buttermilk; but indeed the potatoes they had when I was there were scarce fit for pigs, they were so bad. I was told, however, that they are allowed bread instead of the potatoes during the months of June, July, and August. The three o'clock bell brings them again to work, and the supper bell rings at half past five; the supper consists of two ounces of meal and water, boiled to the consistency of jelly, or paste, and in fact would be of more service in the latter way, than for a man to use as his supper; this they call *skilly,* or in other words *skillagalee.* The six o'clock evening bell again summons them to their cells, where every person must get his vase in hand as soon as the turnkeys appear, when they are each locked up until six o'clock next morning; the prisoners may either get into their hammocks, or walk about the cell whichever they please, as there is no seat, but the ground flags, and I believe the prisoners are locked up in that cold habitation from the time it gets dark in the winter evenings, until it is day-light in the morning, and so strict is the regulation of the jail, that should any one of the prisoners be found conversing with another, during the hours of labour, they are subject to have their supper, or some other part of their victuals kept from them for their offence.

Thus have I given a description of the manner in which I was treated in the jail of Londonderry, and also some little description of the place itself, and its usages: but I had omitted to mention, that no one was allowed to see me, although frequent application was made by my friends. I also requested leave to get my victuals brought to me by my friends; but this also was denied me, although it would have saved the jail allowance. I was not even allowed to send a letter from the place, without reading it to the Governor, and leaving it to him to seal and send away: nor was any letter allowed to come to me without their reading it. I also sent a memorial to the Lord Lieutenant, requesting his Excellency to allow bail to be taken for me, but happened to be liberated before the answer came, which answer was sent on to Belfast; the Governor of the jail having wrote on the back of the letter that I was liberated and lived in Belfast. When I received this letter, I could see by the seal (which was much defaced and by the letter itself, which was tore beside the seal, that it had been subjected to the impertinent curiosity of some person or persons, whether at the post-office, or at the jail, I will not say; but every one to whom I showed the letter, agreed that the seal had been broke: and whether the Government will allow their seals to be broke, and letters searched, is a thing of which I am completely ignorant; at all events, I am well aware had I done the same thing, I would have been proceeded against as a felon. The contents of the letter was as follows:-

G. KERR,

"Your memorial having been laid before his Excellency the Lord Lieutenant, and by his Excellency's commands referred to the Law adviser of the Crown, I am to inform you, that it appears the Government cannot take upon itself to order the Mayor to take bail of you as you solicit, and that application must be made to the Court of King's Bench."

Signed,

Dublin Castle, &c.   "WM. GOSSET."

Now, whoever reads this letter, cannot but see the unlimited stretch of power placed in the hands of the Mayor of Londonderry, a power which he knows well how to use; nevertheless, it is a power which he ought not to be allowed to use, as by this he has the power to arrest who and whom he pleases, if he can give the least plausible excuse that he suspected them of treasonable or seditious purposes. Besides, the Government could not force him to take bail, therefore a person placed in his official capacity, ought to make it his endeavour not to disturb the public peace, but to protect it; and whether he has done so or not at this time, I will leave it to the public and himself to decide, for he well knew, if he could believe the words of *his Orange brother, whom he persecuted, and now is to stand his trial for perjury,* that the Trades Unions are completely unconnected with politics, or any thing that is bad. Or if he could not believe him, he might have been well satisfied, from what exposition was given of their objects, at the late assizes in Londonderry, when the sawyers whom he apprehended, and the others, were all cleared out on every indictment that his inventive imagination could frame against them.

I know that there are persons who will be both base enough and servile enough to approve of the proceedings taken by the authorities against all who dare raise the name of Trades Union; indeed I saw a woful exhibition of this spirit evinced, on my returning from Londonderry, after my liberation from prison. As I had to go by the Strabane rout of road, we stopt our conveyance when proceeding from Strabane, at a place called Newtonstewart, where we went into a house to get some refreshment, and seeing the Londonderry Sentinel lying on the table, I took it up to look over its columns; when, what should present itself to my view, but an extract from the Belfast Chronicle to this effect:- "Mr. George Kerr, Chairman of the late public meeting in Belfast, held for the purpose of petitioning in behalf of the Dorchester convicts, was apprehended on a charge similar to them, by a warrant from the Mayor of Londonderry. The orator," says the Chronicle, "endeavoured to melt Sir Stephen May by a speech, but it was of no avail, as he had to go to Londonderry."

It would appear that the editor of the Belfast Chronicle had either forgot, or wished to retaliate on me; when, as the Scotch song says, "My back was at the wa';" for the well-merited castigation inflicted on him at the hustings that day of the public meeting, as it will be recollected, that I detected and exposed him as vending spurious falsehoods, and sophisticated reasoning to the public; nay, I even went farther, and showed that he was at once as destitute of the principles of common sense, as he was of the principles of the science of Political Economy; and I challenged him then, as I do now, to prove the assertions he published on that day. And as to what he states, regarding my making a speech to melt Sir Stephen May, it is an assertion at once as false as it is unmanly; but an assertion worthy of the Editor of the Chronicle, or the promulgators of falsehood. What I said in the Court-house that day of my apprehension,

was solely in defence of the Trades Unions, to which I belong.
I have already stated that I was apprehended in the Court-house
of Belfast, where I had been listening to the trial of the Coachmakers, the Flax-dressers, and the Printers, neither of which
bodies belonged to the Trades Union, as the men themselves
stated on that day; nevertheless, both the attornies who were
employed against them, and their late employers also thought
so; as in the one case, Mr. Finlay of the Whig Office allowed
his attorney to withdraw the charge against the Printers, under
the pretended plea that he had heard, *as the Attorney stated it,*
the cheering intelligence, that the Derbyshire Unionists had
been defeated by their late employers. It was in consequence
of this and other remarks that were made by the Attorney
Montgomery, on that day, against the Trades Unions; for the
whole of his address was not against the individuals he was
prosecuting, but against the Trades Unionists of Derbyshire, &c.
and therefore, I thought it a great pity, that the Court should be
led astray by the opinions of Attorney Montgomery, in suspect-
ing the men before them on that day, to be connected with the
Trades Union. Although it was evident the Court had erred
in allowing him to descant on Trades Unions, in place of prosecuting the business he had in hand. However, it served to
divert the Court a little, and perhaps was a little gratifying to
Mr. Finlay, the Whig proprietor; and if the Attorney did not
divert a handsome fee from his pocket, he had himself to blame.
I have taken the liberty of adverting to this, as I do not like to
see any set of men badly used, whether they are Unionists or
not; and there are few humane minds who will think, there
was much cheering intelligence in a number of unfortunate men
and women being starved into employment, the remuneration
for which is scarcely adequate to keep soul and body together.

As soon as I was apprehended, I was called up on the table,
when Sir Stephen May asked me if I was in Londonderry lately,
and if I belonged to the Trades Union and several other
questions. To all of which I answered in the affirmative. He
then told me, he had a warrant from Derry for my apprehension.
I then took the liberty of stating, that notwithstanding all that
had been said in the Court that day, against the Trades Union,
that I was the only individual connected with that body, that
had been brought before him on that day, and that none of the
other individuals were connected with the Trades Union, who
had been brought before him. I also stated that no Trades
Unionist had been brought before him since the commencement
of the Union in Belfast, for any misconduct connected with

their trade affairs, and said I was happy, and ever would remain so, in being a Trades Unionist, as their objects and designs were laudable and praiseworthy; and that they were not determined (as had been broadly asserted by the Attorney on that day) to ruin society by charging an exorbitant price for their labour, as the Trades Unionists well know, that if they charge more for their labour than the public are disposed to give, it would have the tendency of ruining their employers and themselves also; and stated likewise, that I was quite willing to take my trial on behalf of the Trades Union at any time, and said I was ready to produce bail for my appearance; but was told by Sir Stephen, that the warrant being from Derry, I had to go there before bail could be accepted.

This is the plain fact, and the reader will see whether the Editor of the Chronicle had any reason to say that I endeavoured to melt Sir Stephen by a speech. However, I certainly think, that if the Editor of the Chronicle has any shame, he ought to feel it in a *melting degree*. I have shown him to be culpable in every point where he assails me. I am not in the habit of calling any man a liar, as it is a harsh ungenteel term; yet if I were as culpable as the Editor of the Belfast Chronicle, I should consider myself a most notorious one. He calls me an orator, by way of irony, I suppose, or perhaps by way of showing his gratitude for the good advice I gave him, and now I have usurped a little on his editorial province, I will be able to shake hands with him, although I have not the honour of editing a Commercial Chronicle; and although his abilities as Editor may be much greater than I can pretend to, still I have the pleasure of telling him that mine could not be much worse than his. But I shall leave him for the present, hoping he will pay more regard to truth, and give me no further occasion to meddle with him, as he may be assured that if he has the hardihood to place himself again in my power, I will give him something tight and handsome.

But I must again recur to my subject, and having depicted already the barbarous and inhumane treatment I received, I cannot close this narration without adverting again to the transactions of the Mayor of Londonderry, and the designs of the greatly abused Trades Unionists. Every one who reads this cannot but see the most determined spirit evinced by the Mayor of Londonderry to punish and harass the Trades Unionists, merely because they were poor; for as I have already remarked, he observed, with a malicious sneer, that the Trades Unionists could not find in all their mighty society, two men to qualify for forty pounds each, thus at once showing that their poverty was as much a crime in his eyes as any thing else, as this was the only remark he made in my presence, that was applicable to their condition; nevertheless, although the Trades Unionists individually are not wealthy; still will they be able to produce from among their ranks, men as talented—men as virtuous—men as humane—men as honest—and *perhaps, men as rich,* as the Worshipful Joshua Gillespie, Esquire, Mayor of Londonderry. Alas! alas! what a pity it is, that poverty should be looked upon as a crime! And again, I cannot but reflect on the manner in which he treated his two Orange brothers, swearing by his immortal God, that he would transport them, if they did not give evidence (against the two others and myself) that we administered an oath to them. Now mark the consistency of such evidence as he wished them to give. The Mayor suspected that they were connected with a secret society, who administered an oath to every member, that they should divulge none of the proceedings of that Society. Now supposing that these men did belong to such a Society (absurd as the supposition is) in the name of common sense could such evidence be relied on? As, in the first place, the individuals themselves were a part of that Society, and consequently as culpable as any member in it; and in the second place, they must perjure themselves by giving evidence, as in the case of the Dorchester men, but yet the law will admit a man's evidence, although he should be a mansworn villain, provided, however, he swear on their side of the question, and the law at the same time will try a man for perjury, should he happen to vary in his statements while they are questioning him. Is there consistency here? Is there a shadow of justice in such legislation? The law of Heaven's great King must be violated, in order to satisfy the caprice or the inclinations of his creatures, who form an earthly tribunal, falsely called by the name of a Court of Justice.

Britons, boast no more of the excellency of your laws; raise not your voices in extolling the freedom of your sons, but cast thine eyes on the gins and snares that your legislators lay to entrap you. Yea, even when you suppose, that you are acting most loyal and upright, the chains and the dungeon are staring you in the face. The Trades Unionists, however, have nothing to fear; they have only obeyed the mandate of the Almighty, by uniting together in the bonds of affection and brotherly love. We know that it has been the unfortunate lot of Ireland to be divided and distorted by faction and party spirit; we know also that the Mayor and the Sheriff of Londonderry, both belong to one of these factions, viz. an Orange Lodge; and perhaps it grieves them to see the Catholics and the Protestants uniting together, for the noblest and the best of purposes, and whether it will be right to hearken unto them, more than to the commands of our Heavenly King—Unionists, judge ye. Act up to your principles, which are based on Christianity, and therefore founded on a rock, which can never be shaken, till mankind shall have forgotten the origin of their being, or the design for which they were created. Unionists, you know that you are assailed by every manner of abuse and persecution; you know that every thing that is bad is laid to your charge, and there are few broils, or altercations between employers and their workmen, but what are laid to the charge of the Trades Unions; therefore, let your public and private conduct show the falseness and maliciousness of the charges. I am compelled to admit that there are bad members connected with the Trades Union; nevertheless, the faults of a few individuals are no more to be laid to our charge, as long as we do not encourage or allow evil, no more than the faults of a few individuals in society at large are to be visited on the Government. For as soon as a man is found to be of a bad character, he ceases from that moment to belong to the Trades Union.

That we conducted our business after the form of Lodges, we never attempted to dispute, or to deny, which certainly never would have been the case, had we not got example from Masonic Lodges, Orange Lodges, Ribbon Lodges, Odd Fellow Lodges, &c.; all of these, if not sanctioned, were at least tolerated by law; and for my part, I never did belong to any Lodge, nor knew nothing of Lodge ceremony, until I was connected with a Trades Union Lodge; and although I know nothing of any other lodge proceedings, still one thing I know, that there can be no lodges more loyal, or more anxious to support and obey the laws of their country, than the Trades Union Lodges. But there never was a time when society began to improve, either their moral, intellectual, religious, or physical condition, when men were a wanting, who were both able and anxious to commit the most horrid acts of atrocity and barbarity, in order to impede the progress of good or noble designs. We have seen, for example, the persecutors of Jesus Christ and his disciples, for propagating and bringing in a system, which even their persecutors could not but admire, and which rendered mankind for ever happy, and truly blessed. We have seen, at the dawn of the reformation, the persecution of the martyrs of Christianity, and the fiends who could look with eager satisfaction and delight on the burning and butchering of their fellow mortals. We have seen the persecutions of the patriots, whose hearts and souls beat high for the love and salvation of their country, viz. a Hampden, a Muir, and several others, who suffered for that cause, which is now the law of the land, and which was hailed so universally by the shouts of the millions. We have seen a Saul of Tarsus, hauling men and women to prison for adhering to that cause, which in a little time, he was about to become the best and most devoted of its teachers. And we will yet see those men who are the present persecutors of the Trades Unions, their best supporters, and their most indefatigable advocates. Yes, and though the plaintive cry of the bereaved wife for her husband, and the pitiful wailings of the little children of the poor Dorchester Unionists, may be allowed to cry on in vain for their tender parents, who may be crossing the wide expanse of ocean with their chains and their shackles clanking dolefully on their pensive ears, beating time to the throbs of sorrowed hearts. Yet is there a God who will protect them, and will avenge in his own due time their wrongs and their oppressions; and although a jury (like theirs) may find a verdict of guilty on the evidence of perjured men; and although a Baron Williams may condemn them to the utmost extent of a cruel and arbitrary statute, which even he himself was doubtful whether the men could be convicted upon: still is there a Judge on high who will hear the appeal of the distressed, and who will let the oppressed go free. For my part, I count it an honour to be in the condition of the unfortunate men; but on the other hand, had I done what Baron Williams has done, I would look upon myself as a dishonoured man for ever, and that I had been guilty of an error which time could neither efface nor obliterate.

My own trial will come on about the 25th July, and conscious as I am of my innocence of the crime laid to my charge, of being an unlawful combinator; yet nothing shall shake my fortitude or daunt my resolution, of bearing manfully and patiently whatever the hand of persecution, or the might of injustice may lay upon me. My life was given me for no other purpose, but to be ever ready to do a good action, or to support a good cause; and if, to promote the improvement of society, by endeavouring all in my humble capacity, to lead the minds of my fellow-workmen to aspire to these lofty ideas which will best promote their own good, and the welfare and approbation of society at large, be constituted a crime, then shall I feel highly honoured in suffering for a good cause, and although the prison or the dungeon may be made the receptacle of my body, making a cursed and a cruel separation between the wife of my bosom and I; and although the little prattling tongues of my dear children, shall have to cry in vain for their papa, yet shall not my spirit humble itself to the tyrant or the oppressor, but in the midst of my suffereings, shall my mind triumph over the cruelty and the nothingness of those who might solace and delight themselves in my affliction; for never shall my children have to say, that their father was a coward, or capable of flinching from his post, when oppression was near.

One word in conclusion to the Trades Unionists. Brothers, let all your actions be guided by that noble-spirited magnanimity of mind which cannot but make your enemies admire you, always holding up to public odium and detestation, those individuals who would violate either the laws of their country or the principles of the Trades Union. Let it not be said, that all your ends are to obtain an exorbitant price for your labour, and whenever you feel yourselves oppressed, endeavour as far as possible, to gain redress by making known your propositions to your employers, being well aware that the interests of both are (or at least ought) to be one. I know well that there are tyrants among employers, and also among the men; but in order to afford no gratification, either to the one or to the other, let your differences be settled by peaceable and concilatory measures; and should you, after this, be dealt injustly with, lay your grievances open to the public, and you will then have a claim upon their sympathy. Having now said this much, I shall beg leave to conclude, and be assured, that neither my hand nor my heart, shall ever be wanting, when the cause of my fellow-workman requires the aid of either, in a just and honourable cause.

Meantime I subscribe myself,

Your Brother in Union,

GEORGE KERR.

APPENDIX II

QUIET RECONCILIATION

BEING an account of the Churches' Industrial Council's (hereafter referred to as C.I.C.) contribution to the healing of the breach between the Government of Northern Ireland and the

Irish Congress of Trade Unions (hereafter referred to as the I.C.T.U.).

1. INTRODUCTION:

In 1958 the C.I.C. felt it must examine the problem of unemployment, particularly in Belfast, where threatened redundancies in both the ship building and aircraft industries suggested the probability of acute social tension and widespread hardship amongst, not only people whose livelihood depended on the two industries but also the numerous shopkeepers, professional men etc; whose businesses were directly linked to full employment in those key industries.

As a result of very careful investigations the Council decided to draw together a group of people, each of whom would represent, officially, a particular sectional interest in the community. We aimed to discover whether we could offer an element of leadership which in turn would enable those drawn together to combat the common enemy—unemployment. Official representatives were eventually nominated from different employers' organisations, the I.C.T.U., the press, radio and T.V., the university, the stock exchange, the Belfast College of Technology and the N.I. Tourist Board. Later, representatives from the Ulster Farmers' Union joined the group, making a total of some 30 members. The C.I.C.'s own chairman agreed to act as chairman of this "consultative and action group" (hereafter referred to as the C and A group) and the C.I.C. appointed a small sub-committee of some four or five members representing the Council to serve on the group. The N.I. Government appointed two observers from the "Economic Advisory Office."

It was at this point that we began to become acutely aware of the problems and frustrations arising from the non-recognition of the I.C.T.U. by the Northern Ireland Government. Our basic philosophy was to awaken the public conscience and then to stimulate a community approach to the fundamental problem of unemployment. 'Self help,' later to become a political catchphrase, was the keystone of our concern and a phrase we constantly used in our discussions with the C and A group. It rapidly became clear however, that any such action must be based upon a solid tripartite foundation—government, employers and trade unions. But the government and the I.C.T.U. were unable to meet together due to the problem of non-recognition. Hence, all our efforts were doomed to failure and the more we talked with the different sections of the community the more this became apparent. At the same time, however, we became aware that there existed a tremendous amount of "latent goodwill" which, if we could tap and release, could prove to be the dynamic we were all seeking. We were particularly impressed by the way in which representatives of employers' organisations privately expressed a deep desire to see healed the breach between the government and the I.C.T.U. After meeting for some twelve months we decided to suspend further meetings whilst the C.I.C. sub-committee tried to penetrate the problem as they saw it and effect a reconciliation between the two parties. Two practical examples of the stultifying effect of non-recognition on the economic growth and stability of the province, which helped to crystallise our own thinking and policy were:-

(a)   The impossibility of setting up a N.I. Productivity Council during "National Productivity Year" sponsored by the Duke of Edinburgh and observed throughout the U.K.

(b)   The abortive attempt in 1963 to establish an "Economic Development" Council designed to foster industrial development in Northern Ireland.

2.   HISTORY OF THE PROBLEM OF NON RECOGNITION:

The Irish Trade Union Congress was formed in 1894 by the Irish membership of unions with headquarters in Great Britain. In 1920 the Government of Ireland Act set up a political framework in which was established the Six-county Government of Northern Ireland and the Twenty-six county Government of Southern Ireland. In 1942 the I.T.U.C. set up a special committee to determine how best trade unionism could function in the political framework of Northern Ireland.

The report to this committee was adopted by annual conference 1943/44 and a Northern Ireland Committee appointed, with the basic functions of considering how Congress decisions would affect members in Northern Ireland, of examining industrial legislation created by the Northern Ireland Government and of liaising with ministers and departments of state in the North, and generally acting as an advisory and consultative body in trade union affairs to the National Executive of the I.T.U.C.

This Northern Ireland Committee then made representations to the Northern Ireland Government to be recognised as the central trade union authority for Northern Ireland. The Government replied, in effect, that whilst wishing to recognise and consult with trade unions in Ulster this would be done through individual unions or, if necessary, through other amalgamations of trade unions, e.g. "The Confederation of Shipbuilding and Engineering" unions.

In 1945 the N.I. Committee of the I.T.U.C. was made a sub-committee of the National Executive of the I.T.U.C. consisting of 10 persons nominated by the N.I. annual conference subject to ratification by the National Executive. The first meeting of this committee discussed how they could obtain recognition by the N.I. Government. Subsequently they enlisted the aid of affiliated organisations in Great Britain to bring pressure to bear on the N.I. Government, but without much success. The government's reply, whilst accepting the principle of recognising and discussing with trade unions, invariably pointed out that they could not recognise a committee whose headquarters were in the Irish Republic and whose "affiliated unions include trade unions operating from headquarters in that country" i.e. the Republic. Such replies also normally referred to the alleged policy of the I.C.T.U. to embrace trade unions operating in Northern Ireland through a "single all-Ireland trade union congress" with the "eventual disappearance of British-based unions from Ireland—North and South."

In 1961 the P.M. refused to receive Mr. W. J. Blease, N.I. Officer I.C.T.U. as one of the elected members of a deputation dealing with unemployment.

From investigations at this time it appeared that the N.I. Government's non-recognition of the N.I. Committee of the I.C.T.U. was based on:

(a) Their head office being located in Dublin.

(b) Their I.C.T.U. constitution affording a majority of seats on the Executive Council to Irish-based unions.

(c) The N.I. Committee being an advisory body only, having no autonomy and thereby subjected to majority rulings from the Republic.

Finally we noted that 85 per cent (i.e. 190,000 members) of trade unions with members in Northern Ireland were affiliated to the I.C.T.U. The remaining 15 per cent were composed of smaller more fragmented unions.

3. C.I.C.'s WORK:

The Council felt it necessary, as a first step, to acquaint itself with as many responsible views on the problem of non-recognition as possible. In October 1962 the C.I.C. requested a meeting with N.I. members at the Westminster Parliament to hear their viewpoint. On 26th October, 1962, five Northern Ireland members from the Imperial Parliament met with the

C.I.C. Apologies were received from all the remaining Imperial M.P.s. Whilst our visitors were extremely cautious they left us in no doubt that they regretted the impasse between Stormont and the I.C.T.U. but could see no alternative as long as their objections (as above) could be levelled at the I.C.T.U. They assured us of their willingness to work for recognition and pledged us their individual support in our efforts to heal the breach.

The C.I.C. decided next to invite a back-bencher, from the N.I. Government, who had been particularly outspoken in his criticism of the I.C.T.U. and who had appeared, in public, to adopt a position *vis-a-vis* the I.C.T.U. of extreme intransigence.

Due to being out of the country at the time this member forwarded us a letter in which he put forward the views he held and which were a fair reflection of reports we had read in the press and of statements made at Stormont. After outlining the background to the situation he drew our attention to the Unionist Party policy outlined in their official booklet, "Forward with Unionism." This stated that the Unionist Party were not prepared to recognise the I.C.T.U. but would recognise a N.I. Committee of the British T.U.C. He pointed out that this firmly pledged his party to a policy of non-recognition and went on to give as his opinion that this was also the majority opinion of trade unionists in Northern Ireland. He saw recognition as a threat to the sovereignty of Northern Ireland as a state and felt that any Northern Ireland Government which recognised the I.C.T.U. would not survive.

On the 4th April, 1963, the C.I.C. wrote to the Government Chief Whip requesting a meeting with Unionist M.P.s. This was agreed provided that M.P.s spoke for themselves and not for the party. On the 7th May three back-benchers met us. There was a full and frank exchange of views, with the M.P.s adopting much the same attitude as the Imperial M.P.s. The only hope they could see was for a linking up of the N.I. Committee with the British T.U.C.

At this time our sub-Committee was also having discussions with other groups in the community about the possibility of an "Economic Advisory Council" for Northern Ireland. Again it became obvious that non-recognition would be the stumbling block. This led our sub-committee to request an interview with the Prime Minister which was eventually arranged for 18th September, 1963. The P.M. was joined by the Ministers of Labour and Commerce, their advisers and the Secretary to the Cabinet.

We explained to the P.M. our background and the nature and conclusions of our investigations. In particular we stressed two factors which we considered of overwhelming importance, namely:-

(1) "that the I.C.T.U. have accepted two fundamental principles that would make "recognition" acceptable, even to some right-wing Unionist members of Parliament. These principles are:

(a) recognition of the Northern Ireland Government, and

(b) autonomy of the Northern Ireland Committee in all trade union affairs in Northern Ireland, provided that action by the Northern Committee in industrial matters did not violate principles adopted by the trade union movement as a whole."

(2) "most of the people that we met seemed to be desperately anxious that the problem should be solved and indeed that the Government of Northern Ireland should work with the I.C.T.U."

We stressed too that responsible trade union leaders might find it difficult to continue to restrain their more militant members who clearly wished to express their disapproval of government policy in a more militant manner. We pointed out the danger of "a hardening of trade union attitude and a decline in confidence of government supporters." We urged:

"(1) A fresh initiative on the part of the Government towards co-operation with the I.C.T.U.

(2) In any re-consideration of the membership of the Economic Council, the declared wishes of the trade union movement represented by the I.C.T.U. should be accepted but that there should also be recognition of the existence of trade unions outside the I.C.T.U., numbering some 30,000 members.

(3) We offered any help that we could give through our many contacts with varied groups in our society, to strengthen the government's hand in any efforts made towards solving the problems on these lines and would be glad of guidance in this direction."

Again there was a frank discussion of our proposals, but whilst expressing sorrow at what he described as a "tragic situation" the P.M. said he felt that public opinion had not changed fundamentally and the people of Northern Ireland did not want the government to recognise the I.C.T.U. The situation would be different if the committee was a branch of the British T.U.C. with headquarters in London. We suggested that we had conclusive evidence of a shift of opinion in the community. The P.M. advised us to place this evidence before the Chief Whip who would need to be convinced.

On the 7th October our sub-committee met with the Northern Ireland Committee to report on our discussions with the P.M. It was decided at this meeting to follow the P.M.'s advice and seek a meeting with the Government Chief Whip and his back-benchers.

We requested this meeting on the 20th September but on the 3rd October we received a letter telling us that the Chief Whip now felt acquainted with our views, having read the minutes of our meeting with the P.M. We had further discussions with the Northern Ireland Committee. We became conscious of tension entering the debate from the trade union side. We were reminded that not all trade unionists in Northern Ireland wanted to co-operate with the government. A threat had already been made public that trade unionists were seriously considering withdrawing their support from those areas where they were co-operating with the government, e.g. training schemes.

It was also felt that unless progress was made the impasse could be the means of turning the trade union movement's attention from economic to political matters, in terms of partition. Yet this was the last thing which the Northern Ireland Committee wanted themselves. They re-emphasised, however, in their public utterances, that the trade union movement in Ireland had always been united and that there would never be any change in this situation. On this they were solidly united.

Our sub-committee left this meeting wondering just how we might help to reconcile two parties apparently in such fundamental conflict. We decided to make a fresh approach to the Chief Whip which we did immediately. After the exchange of three or four letters a meeting was arranged for the 22nd January, 1964, at Stormont. Before this took place we learned that the Executive Council of the I.C.T.U. were to hold their next meeting in Belfast and we asked that they should receive our sub-committee. This was arranged for the 16th December and whilst our attendance was understandably brief it was of immense value because it gave rise to a public statement embracing the following two points:-

(1) Individual unions affiliated to the Northern Ireland Committee would in future be given greater say in the making of general policy.

(2) The executive of the I.C.T.U. appointed a sub-committee to work with the C.I.C. on the issue of recognition.

This meant that we had at last achieved full and official co-operation from one party to the dispute.

On the 20th December we drew up the following formula which we hoped to be able to offer to both the government and the I.C.T.U. as a working compromise. Our concern was to capture the spirit latent in the community as well as both parties to the dispute which favoured a solution. The precise wording was not of paramount importance. Our concern was. The formula read: "Recognising the need for an extension of economic planning policies and accepting the way in which government increasingly impinges on what hitherto were almost exclusively industrial affairs, it is agreed that, for the trade union movement to be in a position to advise on and influence such policies, to the advantage of their members, the Northern Ireland Committee of the I.C.T.U. be empowered to take decisions relating to such policies in Northern Ireland, and to deal directly and authoritatively with the Government of Northern Ireland.

Notwithstanding this the Northern Ireland Committee of the I.C.T.U., naturally, will continue to be free to consult with fellow trade unionists and will continue to play its part in emphasising the fundamental unity of the trade union movement in all industrial matters."

Our sub-committee assembled at Stormont on the 22nd January, 1964, and were introduced by the Chief Whip to twelve Government back-benchers, including three senators. Our concern was to stimulate discussion on the issue of recognition, answer criticisms where possible, and if the opportunity was created circulate our formula for discussion.

The meeting began with one or two back-benchers advancing stereotyped arguments against trade unions in general and the I.C.T.U. in particular. We retaliated with the viewpoint that not only did we represent diverse sections of the community but that we also had a first hand knowledge of the trade union movement and the working of an industrial democracy. We stated clearly that a solution had to be found for the well-being of the community as a whole. This blunt approach proved the turning point because again there became apparent a latent reservoir of good intention and we got down to the real issues of recognition. Ultimately it was agreed that it would be impossible to achieve the complete, absolute autonomy of the N.I. Committee but that any move in this direction would be worth support. This attitude indicated the first step away from the entrenched position of the government as embodied in their various public statements. We were asked to indicate what we had been doing in our discussions in the community and this gave us the chance to circulate our formula. There followed a thorough discussion on the formula which ended with an overwhelming majority of back-benchers accepting it as the sort of statement which would meet their own wishes. We were asked to continue our efforts.

We received a letter from the Chief Whip on the 28th January in which he indicated that our meeting with the back-benchers had been profitable and that he would arrange a further meeting for us should we require it. We were making progress!

On the 7th February we held a further meeting with the N.I. Committee at which we discussed the points raised by the government back-benchers. We went on to discuss the possibility of changing the I.C.T.U. constitution with special reference to Clause 39. The working party felt this would not be possible for two reasons.

(a)   Overtures from the I.C.T.U. had always been rebuffed in the past by the government and they felt unable to recommend any changes which might be rejected by the government.

(b)   It was felt that extremists from both wings of the T.U. movement could create difficulty over the precise wording of an amended constitution.

It was felt that the best approach would be to present to the next annual general meeting of Congress a suitably worded resolution along the lines of our formula.

On the 3rd March we received a letter from the N.I. Officer I.C.T.U. referring to our meeting with his sub-committee and informing us that the Executive Council had decided to investigate, "The full implication to the constitution of Congress of the formula prepared by the C.I.C." This showed a slight but welcome deviation from the working parties attitude to the constitution.

On the 4th March we wrote to the Chief Whip informing him of our meeting with the N.I. sub-committee to which he replied with the following: "I hope very much that you will be successful in your efforts and I shall be glad to arrange for you to have another meeting with our back-benchers when you are ready." Clearly the two parties were drawing closer.

On the 23rd April we were informed by the N.I. Officer during conversation that a memorandum had been drawn up showing how constitutional changes could be made without harming the trade union movement and yet at the same time meeting criticisms which had been made of its constitution.

During all our discussions we were aware, of course, of the work being done by other groups in the community to heal the breach. In particular we were aware of the work done by the Chambers of Commerce and to a lesser degree the National Association of British Manufacturers who were later to receive widespread publicity. We were aware also that both parties had to deal with supporters within their own ranks who opposed reconciliation. On the government side were those who saw reconciliation as appeasement in terms of partition, whilst on the trade union side there were those who saw reconciliation as a threat to their strength in terms of militancy.

On the 25th April we were asked by the N.I. Officer of the I.C.T.U. to withdraw from the situation as his executive had decided to proceed with the constitutional changes irrespective of the N.I. Government's attitude. It was subsequently announced that a meeting between government representatives and the N.I. Committee would be held to discuss recognition on the 30th April. On that day we sent the following telegram to the P.M. and the N.I. Officer, from the C.I.C.

> "Wishing every success to the important discussions today between the government and trade unions. Also for any future meetings involving the economic and industrial well-being of the people of Northern Ireland."

The proposed amendment to the Congress constitution was discussed by Congress at a private session on the 28th July, 1964. C.I.C. sub-committee members were invited to join the platform party as "distinguished visitors" and were hence present at this crucial session. As recorded in the press a resolution was passed by Congress which gave greater autonomy to the Northern Ireland Committee in respect of Northern Ireland affairs and which clearly would pave the way to healing the breach with the government. The relationship between the amendment to the constitution and our original formula is self evident.

The way was now open to finally heal the 21-year-old running sore which had done much damage to the prosperity and economic security of the people of Northern Ireland.

On 29th July we wrote to both the I.C.T.U. and the government congratulating them on the success of their joint working group. The Secretary to the Cabinet replied as follows: "The Prime Minister has asked me to acknowledge with thanks your letter of 29th July concerning the relationship between the Government and the Irish Congress of Trade Unions and to say that he much appreciates the Churches Industrial Council's helpfulness in the past and their good wishes for the future."

4. CONCLUSIONS:

As a council we have learned four simple yet fundamental lessons from the proceeding:

(a) The Church cannot contract out of community social problems no matter how intractable or deep rooted they may appear to be. Indeed the more intractable the problem the more urgent it is that we bring to bear our Christian insights.

(b) In our community there are deep wells of latent goodwill which cut across traditional lines of demarcation in terms of religion and/or social classes. These are the foundations on which the community must build. The Church, if she is to be true to her faith, must and can give the lead in this.

(c) When dealing with this type of complex problem (complex in terms of history, tradition, trade unionism, economics and politics) we Christians must try to be experts in these complexities and must try to deal with them at *their* level, in *their* language and on *their* terms—not as we would like to see the situation.

(d) Throughout this four-year period we went about our business objectively but unobtrusively. Our role was that of quiet reconciliation—of talking behind the scenes and reconciling conflicting viewpoints on the basis of "what is best for the whole community?" This would seem to be the technique we ought, on most occasions, to adopt. We would like to feel that by our lack of vested interests and our quiet but objective persistence we won the trust of both parties to this particular problem to a degree not quite attained by any of the other groups working towards the same goal. If this is true, it places added responsibility on our shoulders for our future activities.

BIBLIOGRAPHY

BOOKS:
ASPINALL, A: *The Early English Trade Unions,* London 1949.
BLANCO, J. P. G: *Protection of Wages,* Geneva 1959
BOYD, ANDREW: *Have the Trade Unions Failed the North?.* Cork 1984.
BOYLE, J. (ed): *Workers and Leaders,* Cork 1966.
CLARKSON, J. D: *Labour and Nationalism in Ireland,* Columbia University 1925.
COLE, G. D. H. and POSTGATE, R: *The Common People,* London 1938.
CONNELLY, T. J: *The Woodworkers,* London 1960.
CONNOLLY, J: *Labour in Ireland,* Dublin 1922; *Labour, Nationality and Religion,* Dublin 1949.
CROUCHER, R: *Engineers at War,* London 1982.
DAVITT, M: *Fall of Feudalism in Ireland,* London and New York 1904.
EDWARDS, O. W: *The Sins of our Fathers,* Dublin.
ENGELS, F: *Conditions of the Working Class in England in 1844,* Moscow 1953.
FISK, R: *The Point of No Return,* London 1975.
FOX, R. M: *History of the Irish Citizen Army,* Dublin 1944; *Louie Bennett,* Dublin; *Jim Larkin,* London 1957.
GAUGHAN, J. A: *Thomas Johnston,* Dublin 1980.
GLESPEN, J. N: *Grattan and his Times,* Dublin 1960.
GREAVES, C. D: *Life and Times of James Connolly,* London 1961.
GREEN, E. R. R: *The Lagan Valley, 1800–1850,* London 1949.
HAMMOND, J. L. & B: *The Bleak Age,* London 1957; *The Town Labourer,* London 1949; *The Village Labourer,* London 1949.
HANNINGTON, W: *Unemployed Struggles,* London 1936.
HIGENBOTTAM, S: *Our Society's History,* Manchester 1939.
INGLIS, B: *The Freedom of the Press in Ireland,* London 1957.
ISLES, K. S. and CUTHBERT, N: *An Economic Survey of Northern Ireland,* H.M.S.O., Belfast 1957.
JEFFREYS, J. B: *The Story of the Engineers,* London 1945.
KENNA, G. B. (Fr. J. HASSAN): *Facts and Figures on the Belfast Pograms, 1920–1922,* Dublin 1922.
KENT, W: *John Burns, Labour's Lost Leader,* London 1950.
LANE, T: *The Union Makes Us Strong,* London 1974.
LARKIN, E: *James Larkin,* London 1965.
LEWIS, A. H: *The Molly Maguires,* London, 1965.
MACARDLE, D: *The Irish Republic,* London 1938.
McDOWELL, R. B: *Irish Public Opinion, 1750–1800,* London, 1954.

MacFarlane, L. J: *The Right to Strike,* London 1981.

Marx, K: *Capital* (Vol. 1), Moscow 1954.

Millar, J. P. M: *The Labour College Movement,* London 1979.

Musson, A. E: *The Typographical Association,* Oxford 1954.

Nevin, D. (ed): *1913: Jim Larkin and the Dublin Lockout,* Dublin 1964; *Trade Unions and Change in Irish Society,* Cork 1980.

O'Brien, G: *Economic History of Ireland* (Vol. III), London 1921.

O'Brien, W: *Forth the Banners Go,* Dublin 1969.

O'Byrne, C: *As I Roved Out,* Dublin.

O'Casey, S: *Drums Under the Windows,* London 1948; *History of the Irish Citizen Army,* Dublin 1914.

O'Connell, M: *Irish Politics and Social Conflict in the Age of the American Revolution,* Philadelphia 1965.

Prior, J., Benn, T. and Murray, L: *The Role of the Trade Unions,* London 1980.

Pritt, D. N. and Freeman, R: *The Law versus the Trade Unions,* London 1958.

Read, D. and Glasgow, E: *Fergus O'Connor,* London 1961.

Riordan, E. J: *Modern Irish Trade and Industry,* London 1920.

Roney, F: *Irish Rebel and Labour Leader,* California 1924.

Rossa, O'Donovan: *My Years in English Jails,* Tralee 1967.

Ryan, W. F: *The Irish Labour Movement,* Dublin 1919.

Schoyen, A. R: *The Chartist Challenge,* London 1958.

Sexton, J: *Sir James Sexton, Agitator,* London 1936.

Sheehy-Skeffington, F: *Michael Davitt,* London 1908.

Shillman, B: *Trade Unions and Trade Disputes in Ireland,* Dublin 1960.

Strauss, E: *Irish Nationalism and British Democracy,* London 1951.

Swift, J: *History of the Dublin Bakers and Others,* Dublin 1948.

Vester, H. and Gardner, A: *Trade Unions and the Law,* London 1955.

Webb, B. and S: *History of Trade Unionism,* London 1920

Webb, J. J: *The Guilds of Dublin,* Dublin 1929.

— *Attempt to Smash the ITGWU,* Dublin 1924

— *Documents of the First International,* London 1964

— *Fifty Years of Liberty Hall, 1909–1959,* Dublin 1959.

PAMPHLETS:

Boyle, J: *The Rural Labourer,* Belfast, 1959; *The Belfast Protestant Association and the Independent Orange Order,* 1901–10.

Getgood, R: *Development of Irish Trade Unionism,* Belfast 1944.

Kerr, G: *Exposition of Legislative Tyranny and Defence of the Trade Union,* Belfast 1834.

LARKIN, E: *Socialism and Catholicism in Ireland*, Mass. 1965.

LAW, R: *The Moral Duties Necessary to Secure the Advantages of Free Trade*, Dublin 1780.

MCGLADDERY, D. R: *The Irish Congress of Trade Unions: A Unionist Viewpoint*, Belfast 1963.

Belfast and District Trades Council: A Short History, Belfast 1951.

Constitution of the Irish Congress of Trade Unions, Dublin 1959.

Draft Constitution for a Trade Union Centre for Ireland, PUTUO, Dublin 1957.

First Report of Provisional United Organisation, Dublin 1956.

Joint Memorandum on Trade Union Unity, Dublin 1954.

Quiet Reconciliation, Churches Industrial Council, Belfast 1965.

N. Ireland, Blueprint for Prosperity, NABM, Belfast, 1962.

Repeal the Trade Disputes Act, Irish TUC, Belfast 1957.

Report of Special Delegate Conference, CIU, Dublin 1945.

Second Report of Provincial United Organisation, Dublin 1957.

The Facts Concerning Larkin's Departure to America, Dublin 1924.

THESES:

BLEAKLEY, D. W: *Trade Union Beginnings in Belfast and District*, Belfast 1955.

BOYLE, J. W: *The Rise of the Irish Labour Movement, 1887–1907*, Dublin 1960.

D'ARCY, F: *Dublin Artisan Activity, Opinion and Organisation, 1820–1850*, Dublin 1968.

HARBINSON, J. F: *History of Northern Ireland Labour Party, 1891–1949*, Belfast 1966.

HOLOHAN, P: *Daniel O'Connell and Trade Unions*, Cork 1968.

MONAGHAN, J. J: *A Social and Economic History of Belfast, 1790–1800*, Belfast 1936; *1801–1825*, Belfast 1940.

MISCELLANEOUS

BINKS, J. H: *Presidential Address*, Cork 1956; *Chairman's Address*, Belfast 1958.

BLEAKLEY, D. W: *The Northern Ireland Trade Union Movement*, Belfast 1954.

BOYLE, J. W: *The Irish Labour Movement, 1880–1907*, Paris 1961.

O'CONNELL, M. R: *Class Conflict in a Pre-Industrial Society: Dublin in 1780*. Montreal 1963.

O'GRADA, C: *Karl Marx and the Irish*, Dublin 1970.

O'HIGGINS, R: *Irish Trade Unions and Politics, 1830–50. The Irish Chartists of Barnsley. The Irish Influence in the Chartist Movement*. London 1961.

INDEX